THE
BRIDE'S
Etiquette
GUIDE

ETIQUETTE MADE EASY

Second Edition

Pamela A. Lach

CHICAGO
REVIEW
PRESS

Library of Congress Cataloging-in-Publication
Lach, Pamela A., 1954–
    The bride's etiquette guide / Pamela A. Lach.
        p.   cm.
    Includes index.
    ISBN 978-1-55652-940-5
    1. Wedding etiquette. 2. Etiquette for women. I. Title
BJ2051.L29 1998   98-18501
395.2'2—dc21

A variety of names have been used for the purpose of providing examples. Any similarity to actual people is purely coincidental.

Cover design: Visible Logic
Cover photo: Alexandra Grablewski / Botanica / Jupiterimages
Interior design: Jonathan Hahn

Published by Chicago Review Press, Incorporated
814 North Franklin Street
Chicago, IL 60610
ISBN 978-1-55652-940-5
Printed in the United States of America
5 4 3 2 1

Contents

Introduction

This book is for every bride who is overwhelmed by all the questions that she must answer; befuddled by the countless decisions that she must make; and frustrated by the contradictory and sometimes self-serving advice that she receives.

That's you, isn't it? You genuinely want to come up with the right answers and make suitable decisions. Yet you don't have time to wade through a huge book every time a question arises, especially when your life and your wedding plans don't necessarily fit a perfect traditional mold.

You need a bridal etiquette book because you only get married once—well, hopefully. There are traditions, customs, and practices that apply to a wedding celebration that are unfamiliar to you. There is no reason that you should know all of the answers. Planning a wedding has not been part of your daily life until now.

Even the simplest wedding requires you to choose among options, answer questions, and prepare a plan. You need this source at your fingertips to guide you through the tangled network of information.

So how do I know so much about weddings? Over the years, I've written four other wedding-related books. I learned about weddings the hard way: by attending and participating in them. After I saw the many fiascoes that occurred at those weddings, other people asked me to help them avoid such problems. Then their friends and relatives wanted assistance, too. I wrote down practical and realistic advice for wedding planning, saving money, writing thank-you notes, and surviving the initial years of marriage.

An acquaintance, who didn't know that some of my books were about this topic, was speaking about a recent wedding that we attended. Someone (not me) mentioned that the bride could have used a good etiquette book. The acquaintance responded, "Who cares about etiquette nowadays? Who needs to be told what to do by some stuffy prune wearing white gloves and a flowered hat?"

You can imagine how I loved that comment! Actually I'm wearing jeans as I write this, and I'm neither prim nor pompous. And I haven't worn white gloves or a flowered hat since I was six years old.

From now on your wedding planning will be easier in many ways. This book is organized into twelve chapters. Each chapter discusses a large variety of questions and concerns and suggests traditional answers and solutions and adapts well-established customs to more modern situations. In addition, a glossary explains common and confusing terms you may encounter. In this newly revised edition, I have added information on save-the-date notices, destination weddings, and wedding Web sites. Chapter 8 is a primer on manners to help get you through all the introductions, gatherings, and dinners — you'll feel relaxed, confident, and ready to apply the basic etiquette principles to any special situations or unique circumstances that relate to your wedding. And finally, in the back of the book, you will find a helpful index.

1

Getting Engaged

"How long is a traditional engagement?"

That depends on the style of your wedding. A more formal wedding, with a large wedding party and guest list, takes longer to plan. Your religious denomination is another factor to consider, as many require a premarital counseling period that can last up to one year. The availability of the reception hall and caterer could influence when you get married. During the peak wedding months of June, July, and August, popular locations might already be reserved two years ahead of time. The date you and your fiancé choose should take into consideration the availability of the reception hall and the caterer to allow you to have the type of wedding that you desire.

"Whom do I tell first?"

You should tell both sets of parents, no matter what your age. If they have never met your fiancé, and you live too far away for a meeting to be practical, at least introduce him by phone. Ideally, your parents and fiancé have already met. If they are unable to meet in person, your parents should then write your fiancé a letter welcoming him to the family.

"What if he insists we tell his family first? I want to tell mine first. We can't be in two places at once unless we each do it alone. Is that the best compromise?"

No. Marriage is all about compromise, but you should tell your parents together unless you are expecting a negative reaction. Traditionally the bride's parents are told first.

"My parents dislike my fiancé, and I'm afraid they will say things that will destroy any hope of a future

relationship. Should I still have him there when I tell them?"

If you have a situation where a parent may say something offensive or disagreeable when you tell them the news, it might be better for their child to speak to them alone at first.

"What if I'm closer to someone else? I'm closer to my sister than I am to my mother. Is there any reason I shouldn't tell my sister about the engagement first?"

Traditionally you tell the people who brought you into this world first. Then you tell your siblings, grandparents, aunts, uncles, close friends, and cousins.

"When do I tell my children?"

Children should be among the first to know. They should definitely know before a former spouse knows. You, the parent, should tell the child, ideally alone, so he or she may raise any fears or concerns out of hearing range of your future spouse.

"What if we are in our late forties? Do we still need to tell our parents first?"

You should tell both sets of parents, no matter what your age.

"Should I tell my former spouse?"

It's considerate to personally inform a former spouse of your plans to remarry.

Ring Etiquette

**"Must I have an engagement ring? My mother insists
that without one we aren't really engaged."**

A wedding ring is considered necessary in a matrimonial service. Many women marry without ever receiving an engagement ring. It's a nice betrothal gift, an outward sign that the couple intends to marry, but nothing more.

"Does it have to be a diamond ring?"

No. A diamond is traditional, but you can choose any precious or semiprecious stone that appeals to you.

**"I want to choose my own ring. My fiancé insists that
he's supposed to do it and present it to me. Who's right?"**

You are. Presenting the ring adds high drama to movies and novels. But in reality, most women wish to choose the ring that they will be wearing every day for the rest of their lives. Many couples go to the jeweler together. If your fiancé is budget conscious, he might visit the jeweler beforehand to discuss his budget, asking that only rings in a predetermined price range be presented for your inspection.

"When may I begin wearing my engagement ring?"

As soon as you become engaged and obtain a ring. The man usually presents the ring to the woman privately.

"Are there circumstances where I might wear it on my right hand?"

Yes. Wearing the engagement ring on the right hand is a tradition of some cultures.

"When do we purchase our wedding rings?"

Rings are usually purchased during the engagement.

"Isn't my fiancé supposed to have a ring?"

No. Traditionally the woman receives a ring as part of the marriage ceremony. Customs for men having a ring vary among generations, cultures, and individuals. Men rarely receive engagement rings. It has become more customary for them to wear a wedding ring, but some still consider it optional. But he is just as married with or without the ring.

"Who pays for the wedding rings?"

The rings are gifts. The bride's rings (engagement and wedding) are purchased by the groom. For double-ring ceremonies, the bride purchases the groom's wedding ring.

"Should the rings be engraved?"

This is a matter of individual choice. If engraving is chosen, it is usually the initials and the wedding date. If you select wider bands, you can include a short, meaningful poetic line.

"What should I do with my engagement ring when I walk down the aisle to be married?"

Most brides move the ring to their right hand, then return it to their left hand (on top of the wedding band) after the ceremony.

Announcing the Engagement

"How do I officially announce our engagement?"

Formally, you announce it through the newspaper, mailed announcements, and an engagement party. Informally, you tell family beginning with both sets of parents.

"What if my divorce isn't final yet? Should I wait until the final decree?"

Yes, you should wait until your final divorce decree. It's just not right to announce your engagement while you are still married to someone else.

"Why should we announce our engagement in the newspapers?"

This is the way you let everyone know about the upcoming happy event. It's the best way to inform your many acquaintances who won't be invited to the various festivities.

"When should we notify the newspaper?"

Newspaper announcements usually appear three to six months before the wedding date. Some newspapers have explicit rules about the time lapse between the two, so check your newspaper's policy by calling the society or features editor.

"Would I still announce my engagement if I'm divorced?"

This is generally a personal decision. If your previous marriage took place just a few years before or if you have several children, you may wish just to inform your friends and family in a more quiet fashion. But there's nothing wrong with announcing the news if you wish to do so.

"May I announce my engagement if I'm a widow?"

The purpose of announcing the marriage is to let every friend and acquaintance know about it. Your remarrying is certainly not an insult to your first husband, so why would announcing the marriage be wrong?

"My father is seriously ill. Should we still announce our engagement?"

Traditionally, public announcements are avoided during times of death or serious illness in the immediate family. Instead, the news is spread by word of mouth.

"In whose name is the announcement presented?"

The bride's family traditionally announces the engagement. They notify their local newspaper and the local newspaper for the groom's family. Often the couple lives in an entirely different third location. In this case the bride or her parents would handle the announcement there.

"What about including a photograph with the announcement?"

If you wish for a picture to appear, you will probably need a glossy black-and-white photograph of either you or both of you to accompany the form. It is customary to have this photo taken by a professional photographer.

"What information is included in the traditional announcement?"

Foster & Reed

Mr. and Mrs. Michael Dean Foster of Northbrook, Illinois, announce the engagement of their daughter Hannah Joy Foster to Justin Tyler Reed of Madison, Wisconsin. He is the son of Mr. and Mrs. David Carter Reed of Omaha, Nebraska.

A June 2014 wedding is planned.

Miss Foster was graduated from the University of Illinois at Chicago and is director of marketing with OneRay Corporation of Chicago. Mr. Reed was graduated from the Illinois Institute of Technology and is a freelance civil engineer.

Bride's parents divorced, option 1:

McLeod & Jenkins

Mrs. Emily Polk McLeod of Ann Arbor, Michigan, announces the engagement of her daughter Nicole Marie to Timothy Reilly Jenkins, also of Ann Arbor. Miss McLeod is also the daughter of Mr. James David McLeod of Washington, D.C. Mr. Jenkins is the son of Mr. and Mrs. Reilly Jenkins of Phoenix, Arizona.

An April 2014 wedding is planned.

Miss McLeod was graduated from the University of Michigan and is an economics instructor at Albion College in Albion, Michigan.

Mr. Jenkins graduated from Michigan State University. He is a financial analyst for Kellogg's in Battle Creek, Michigan.

Bride's parents are divorced, option 2:

McLeod & Jenkins

Mrs. Emily Polk McLeod of Ann Arbor, Michigan, and Mr. James David McLeod of Washington, D.C., announce the engagement of their daughter Nicole Marie to Timothy Reilly Jenkins, also of Ann Arbor. Mr. Jenkins is the son of Mr. and Mrs. Reilly Thomas Jenkins of Phoenix, Arizona.

An April 2014 wedding is planned.

Miss McLeod was graduated from the University of Michigan and is an economics instructor at Albion College in Albion, Michigan.

Mr. Jenkins was graduated from Michigan State University. He is a financial analyst for Kellogg's in Battle Creek, Michigan.

Bride's mother has remarried:

Kohler & Daecher

Mr. and Mrs. Andrew Chenzira of Las Vegas, Nevada, announce the engagement of Mrs. Chenzira's daughter

Madeline Rose Kohler to Nicholas Allen Daecher, also of Las Vegas. Miss Kohler is also the daughter of Mr. Ethan Daniel Kohler of San Diego, California. Mr. Daecher is the son of Mr. and Mrs. Christopher John Daecher of Lawton, Oklahoma.

An October 2015 wedding is planned.

Miss Kohler was graduated from Syracuse University and is assistant to the convention director for the City of Las Vegas.

Mr. Daecher was graduated from the University of Oklahoma and is program director for WMWI in Las Vegas.

Bride's mother and father are divorced and both remarried:

Kohler & Daecher

Mr. and Mrs. Andrew Chenzira of Las Vegas, Nevada, announce the engagement of Mrs. Chenzira's daughter Madeline Rose Kohler to Nicholas Allen Daecher, also of Las Vegas. Miss Kohler is also the daughter of Mr. and Mrs. Ethan Daniel Kohler of San Diego, California. Mr. Daecher is the son of Mr. and Mrs. Christopher John Daecher of Lawton, Oklahoma.

An October 2015 wedding is planned.

Miss Kohler was graduated from Syracuse University and is assistant to the convention director for the City of Las Vegas.

Mr. Daecher was graduated from the University of Oklahoma and is program director for WMWI in Las Vegas.

Bride's mother is deceased, father not remarried:

Alvarez & Luna

Mr. Carlos Alvarez of Hartford, Connecticut, announces the engagement of his daughter Ashley Marie Alvarez to Caleb Joel Luna of Stamford. Miss Alvarez is also the daughter of the late Amelia Burkeston Alvarez. Mr. Luna is the son of Mr. and Mrs. Daniel Holton Luna, also of Hartford.

A December 2013 wedding is planned.

Miss Alvarez was graduated from the University of Arizona and is a registered nurse at University Center Hospital.

Mr. Luna was also graduated from the University of Arizona and is curator for the DuPere Historical Museum in Stamford.

Bride's mother is deceased, father remarried:

Alvarez & Luna

Mr. and Mrs. Carlos Alvarez of Hartford, Connecticut, announce the engagement of his daughter Ashley Marie

Alvarez to Caleb Joel Luna of Stamford. Miss Alvarez is also the daughter of the late Amelia Burkeston Alvarez. Mr. Luna is the son of Mr. and Mrs. Daniel Holton Luna, also of Hartford.

A December 2013 wedding is planned.

Miss Alvarez was graduated from the University of Arizona and is a registered nurse at University Center Hospital.

Mr. Luna was also graduated from the University of Arizona and is curator for the DuPere Historical Museum in Stamford.

Bride's father is deceased, mother not remarried. Groom's parents divorced:

Patel & McCoy

Mrs. Noah Patel of Richmond, Virginia, announces the engagement of her daughter Rihanna Elizabeth Patel to Timothy James McCoy of Alma, Michigan. Miss Patel is also the daughter of the late Mr. Noah Patel. Mr. McCoy is the son of Mr. James Tyler McCoy, also of Alma, and Mrs. Ronald Luke Johnson, of Lansing, Michigan.

An April 2014 wedding is planned.

Miss Patel was graduated from Michigan State University and is an administrative assistant at Koerler Rhien Industries.

Mr. Collins was graduated from Central Michigan University and will be relocating to the Richmond area.

Bride's father is deceased, mother remarried. Groom's parents divorced:

Patel & McCoy

Mr. and Mrs. Richard Daniel Olsen of Richmond, Virginia, announce the engagement of Mrs. Olsen's daughter Rihanna Elizabeth Patel to Timothy James McCoy of Alma, Michigan. Miss Patel is also the daughter of the late Mr. Noah Patel. Mr. McCoy is the son of Mr. James Tyler McCoy, also of Alma, and Mrs. Ronald Luke Johnson, of Lansing, Michigan.

An April 2014 wedding is planned.

Miss Patel was graduated from Michigan State University and is an administrative assistant at Koerler Rhien Industries.

Mr. Collins was graduated from Central Michigan University and will be relocating to the Richmond area.

Groom's father is deceased, mother not remarried:

Harvey & Yoder

Mr. and Mrs. Anthony Richard Harvey of Green Bay, Wisconsin, announce the engagement of their daughter Melissa Kay to Joseph Charles Yoder of Milwaukee. Mr. Yoder is the son of Mrs. Allison Violet Yoder of Madison and the late Mr. Kevin Patrick Yoder.

A July 2014 wedding is planned.

Miss Harvey was graduated from the University of

Wisconsin and teaches economics at Griffith High School in Milwaukee.

Mr. Yoder was also graduated from the University of Wisconsin. He is a systems analyst for Altoona Systems in Milwaukee.

Bride is widowed or divorced. Her parents announce the engagement:

Bianchi & Faure

Mr. and Mrs. Sean Neal of Aspen, Colorado, announce the engagement of their daughter Brooke Hailey Bianchi to Devin Brady Faure of Taos, New Mexico. He is the son of Mr. and Mrs. Dillon Lee Faure of Dallas, Texas.

A February 2014 wedding is planned.

Miss Bianchi is an emergency medical technician with Prompt Ambulance Service in Taos.

Mr. Faure was graduated from the Ball State University in Muncie, Indiana, and teaches biology at Rodgers Elementary in Taos.

Bride announces engagement:

Delaney & Tanaka

The engagement of Ms. Grace Isabelle Delaney of Merrillville, Indiana, to Mr. Aiden Taylor Tanaka of Chicago, Illinois, has been announced.

A January 2013 wedding has been planned.

Ms. Delaney was graduated from DePaul University and is a freelance event planner.

Mr. Tanaka was graduated from Michigan State University and is a quality control manager for U.S. Steel.

Groom's parents announce the engagement:

Winthrop & Zavacky

The engagement of Natalie Jane Winthrop, daughter of Mr. and Mrs. Ronald L. Winthrop of Mackinac Island, Michigan, to Jeremy Tyler Zavacky, son of Mr. and Mrs. Robert M. Zavacky Jr., of Valparaiso, Indiana, is announced.

A September 2014 wedding is planned.

Miss Winthrop was graduated from the University of Chicago and is director of Biophysics Laboratories in Northbrook, Illinois.

Mr. Zavacky was also graduated from the University of Chicago and is owner of eleven sports franchises in the Chicago area.

The Engagement Celebration

"What kinds of engagement parties are there?"

Engagement parties are usually simple celebrations, along the lines of a cocktail—or cake and punch—gathering. Some prefer a more formal dinner. In truth, you can do whatever you like. There are no hard-and-fast rules.

"When should the engagement party be held?"

After you become engaged but before it appears in the newspapers.

"Who gives the party?"

Traditionally the bride's family gives the party. However, since so many couples come from different regions, often the groom's family also has a celebratory gathering as a way to introduce the bride to their family and friends. Some couples even throw one for themselves.

"Who should be invited?"

Generally it's a small celebration among close friends and relatives.

"Will we receive gifts?"

Whether you have a party or not, few people give engagement gifts. They are not expected, although a few people close to you may wish to give you one. They are usually items for your new life together, such as linens, paintings, sculptures, and figurines. If some guests have brought gifts and others have not, do not open them at the party. Wait until later and thank them privately.

"Who makes the official announcement at the party?"

Most often the parents propose a toast to the new couple and welcome the new son (or daughter) into the family. Or you can make the announcement together.

2

Wedding Beginnings

Defining Your Wedding Style

"What makes a wedding formal? Semiformal?
Informal?"

Formal

More than 200 guests. Traditional plain invitations. Up to 12 attendants each. Bride in long white gown with train. Groom in cutaway or tailcoat. Ceremony and reception in large, splendid, well-decorated surroundings. Sit-down or buffet-style catered dinner.

Semiformal

Between 75 and 200 guests. Less traditional invitations. Between four and six attendants each. Bride in long gown, anywhere from tea-length to floor-length. Groom in tuxedo. Ceremony and reception in less opulent surroundings. Dinner is buffet, or hors d'oeuvres and sandwiches.

Informal

Fewer than 75 guests. Invitations may be handwritten, computer-generated, or telephoned. Between two and four attendants each. Bride in cocktail-length dress, suit, or very simple long gown. Groom in suit or sports jacket. Ceremony and reception in simple surroundings. Dinner in restaurant or made by friends and relatives; or perhaps just hors d'oeuvres, sandwiches, or cake and punch.

Destination Weddings

This is when couples marry in a distant, beautiful location and invite friends and family to join them. With scattered families it's a way of gathering and enjoying several days of companionship in a lovely locale.

"What are some difficulties in planning this type of wedding?"

It's a little more difficult to organize long distance. You must learn the legal requirements (residency, medical, etc.); find a location for the ceremony and reception; and hire an officiant along with other service providers. In more exotic locations it's almost crucial that you hire a reliable wedding planner.

"Must I pay for all of my attendant's expenses?"

Traditionally the bride and groom cover lodging for out-of-town attendants. For this type of wedding it's probable that all of your attendants will be from somewhere else. If you can afford to pay travel and/or meal expenses, you can choose to provide that as well. If not, there may be some who will be unable to join your wedding party. Be sure to keep communication clear to avoid any misunderstandings. Before you officially ask, make sure they understand the location of the wedding and what expenses they will incur.

"I don't know if any of my family will be able to travel to our destination. What should I do?"

Choosing this option will automatically limit your guest list and expected attendance. It's something to weigh carefully when making your decision. If you can afford to cover their expenses, it would be kind to offer. If not, you must prioritize. What is more important—location or the people beside you?

"How far in advance should I send save-the-date cards? I want to make sure as many people can join us as possible."

There are some companies that require employees to select vacation dates a year in advance. Most prefer six months of notice. Send your cards 12–14 months ahead of time if you can. The sooner the better, especially if you are marrying during a holiday or in an exotic locale.

"Can I put the address of my wedding Web site on the save-the-date card?"

It's a great idea and an ideal way to keep them informed of the plans. If a guest is not internet savvy, however, you should mail information to them.

"Can we have a reception when we return home for those that weren't able to travel?"

Yes. If you had a reception on the same day as your ceremony, you can have a second reception when you return home. If you didn't have a reception that day, the party would be designated as a belated reception.

"How do I make it clear that I can't pay for guests' meals except at the wedding reception?"

There are those who are confused by the situation and assume that there will be meals provided for them throughout their stay.

You might provide a calendar or schedule of activities. Any meals or activities that you are not paying for can be designated "free time" for guests.

"We can pay all expenses for our guests. How do I politely let them know?"

Send a note explaining the plan. The key words to include would be: "our guest" and "all-inclusive trip." Those indicate that you are taking responsibility for expenses. Here's an example:

Dear Aunt Liz and Uncle Rick,

Josh and I will be married June 12, 2015, at Mackinac Island, Michigan. We would like you to join us as our guest for an all-inclusive three day trip. Please save the dates of June 11–13! You can visit our wedding Web site at www. wewillmarry.com for additional information.

I will call you in a few weeks to confirm that you can join us. I must know by November 1 so I can purchase tickets and reserve the hotel room. I am looking forward to spending more time with you during this wonderful celebration!

Best wishes,
Katie

The Wedding Party

"How do I know how many attendants to choose?"

Your personal preference and the size and style of wedding are the foundations for the decision. Traditionally very formal weddings have up to twelve attendants each. Less formal, or semiformal, six to eight each; informal, two to four each; and very small informal celebrations, one attendant each.

"What is the minimum number of attendants we should have?"

Two witnesses to the ceremony to sign the marriage license.

"Whom do we ask?"

Choose people you can rely on, wish to celebrate with, and make an integral part of your day. Usually it's a combination of close friends and family.

"Must I include members of my family?"

Traditionally the choice is yours. However in some cultures you are expected to include siblings and even cousins. In most families there may be some hard feelings if you don't include a few members in your entourage. This is especially true when it comes to siblings. Even if you don't feel particularly close to any of them, it's a good idea to at least talk about your decision if you plan to exclude them.

"Must I include members of my future spouse's family?"

Often if the groom has a sister, the bride includes her as a bridesmaid. If the bride has a brother, the groom might ask him to be a groomsman.

"When do we ask them?"

Ask them after the engagement is announced, but before any official engagement party is held or notices are published. It's a good idea to invite all of your attendants in the same week. This avoids any feeling that one might have that they are a "second choice."

"How do we invite them?"

It's best if you can ask them in person, although a telephone call is an acceptable substitute. Writing them a letter is OK, but might seem a little formal. However it is still wrong to do it through an e-mail, IM, or text message. Those formats diminish the importance of the honor.

"If I was in their wedding, must I ask them to be in mine?"

No, you are not obligated to reciprocate.

"Must the number of bridesmaids and groomsmen be equal?"

No, but it shouldn't be severely unbalanced. A wedding party with eight bridesmaids and two groomsmen would look unusual.

"Do we have to include an attendant's spouse in the wedding party?"

No, it is not necessary. However, the spouses of all your attendants would be invited to the rehearsal dinner, wedding ceremony, and reception.

"I asked an old friend to be in my wedding, and she said 'no thank you.' Should I be insulted?"

Participating in a wedding requires a lot of time and money. In addition to the duties, there is special clothing and gifts to buy, parties to attend, and often travel and transportation expenses too. Not everyone is able to participate in such activities. I wouldn't be insulted. It's better to ask and have them opt out than to assume they can't and hurt their feelings.

"I would like to include my sons in the wedding. Is there any reason that I shouldn't?"

Their role should be minimal, especially if their other birth parent is still alive. Children tend to have mixed emotions at such occasions. You might have them walk with you up to the altar and then sit down with the other close family members.

"What is an honor attendant?"

The term honor attendant replaces the term maid or matron of honor if the bride chooses a male for that role. The same is true if a groom chooses a female friend to fill the role traditionally held by a best man.

"May I have more than one honor attendant?"

Yes, although more than two can cause confusion. The honor attendant has a lot of responsibilities. You don't want a situation where each is assuming that the other is doing the required duties. If you chose two, make sure there is clear and open communication about who will be fulfilling which roles. Remember, you still must choose between them—only one can sign the registry certificate.

"What is the difference between the maid and matron of honor?"

A maid is not, and never has been married. A matron is or has been married.

"What should I consider when choosing a maid or matron of honor?"

You should choose a person you feel very comfortable with, because they will be by your side a great deal before and during the wedding. Ideally you would pick someone who is responsible and reliable, because the duties involved have a significant impact on the wedding.

"I've just learned that my matron of honor will be about eight months pregnant at the wedding. Any suggestions?"

You might choose to have two honor attendants. That will take some of the load off your current matron of honor. The second attendant can also serve as a backup if your friend has her baby early!

"May I ask my mother to be my honor attendant?"

No, as the official hostess of the wedding, she'll have too many other responsibilities.

"Should all the female attendants be the same general age?"

The custom of the wedding attendants being near the age of the bride evolved for practical reasons. They are her support system, and it's logical that attendants much older or much younger may not provide the support the bride needs. Once you have several people to assist you as needed there is no reason why you can't choose someone much younger if you wish.

"Why aren't married bridesmaids called bridesmatrons?"

Although the distinction is made for the honor attendant (maid of honor, matron of honor), it's not made for the other attendants. No matter what their marital status, they are bridesmaids.

"What is a junior bridesmaid?"

A young girl from 10 to 14 years of age. She can dress the same as the other bridesmaids or slightly different. It's entirely optional whether you would assign a groomsman to escort her.

"What is the minimum age for a ring bearer or flower girl?"

Children participating in the wedding shouldn't be younger than four. Younger children tend to become confused and frightened by all the excitement and attention.

"What is the maximum age for a ring bearer or flower girl?"

After the age of 10, the child would be an usher or junior bridesmaid.

"Must I have a ring bearer and a flower girl?"

No. They are traditional but not necessary. They add a cute touch to the day, but both roles are entirely ceremonial.

"What is a page?"

When the bride's gown has an extremely long train, young boys between the ages of four and ten help to carry it in the processional.

"What must the groom consider when choosing a best man?"

He should select someone who will provide help and support as needed, especially on the day of the wedding. Traditionally this person hosts a bachelor party and makes a toast at the reception. He might consider who would best handle those duties when making his selection.

"Can my fiance's father be his best man?"

Yes. He'll probably be honored, and he should be very reliable in that role.

"What is the difference between an usher and a groomsman?"

The roles are often combined, especially in smaller gatherings. By definition the usher hands out programs and seats guests at the wedding ceremony, then lays the aisle runner before the processional. The groomsmen escort the bridesmaids in the processional and recessional and stand with the groom during the ceremony.

"How many ushers do we need if we are expecting 150 guests at our ceremony?"

You can assume that one-half to three-fourths of your invited guests will attend the ceremony. It is best to have one usher for every 50 guests, so in this case you would want to have three ushers.

What to Wear

Bride Attire

Your selection should be based on time of day, location, and formality of the occasion. The style of your dress or gown will determine what everyone else will wear.

"What should I wear to a formal daytime wedding?"

A white or ivory floor-length gown with a long train. If the gown is sleeveless or short-sleeved, wear long gloves. Traditionally a long veil is also worn.

"A formal evening wedding?"

After 6 P.M. the style of clothing would be similar to the above. However, the fabrics are more elegant and the ornamentation more elaborate.

"A semiformal wedding?"

The gown can still be ankle or floor length. Fabrics are less sophisticated and decorations are less detailed. The train (if any) is quite short, and the veil is seldom longer than the elbow.

"An informal wedding?"

Simpler in style, the suit or dress would have minimal lace, embroidery, or other decoration. Often it's the type of outfit you can wear again because it doesn't scream "wedding." Traditional length is slightly below the knee. An ankle length dress in a basic style and fabric would also be acceptable.

"Can I wear a strapless dress to a church wedding?"

A strapless gown, or one that reveals too much in the bust or back area, is not appropriate for a church wedding. Some allow you to cover the area with a light shawl.

"Can I wear a dress that isn't white or ivory?"

Formal weddings are still limited to white or ivory. The more informal, the more colorful the dress can be. Black is still seen as a color of mourning in the United States, and is considered both bad luck and inappropriate for brides.

"Must I wear a veil if I have a church wedding?"

Unless it's a requirement of your particular church, you don't have to wear a veil. Your wedding style, attire, and personal prefer-ence allow you to make the decision.

"What length of veil would I wear with a knee-length dress?"

If your dress is knee length, the veil shouldn't be longer than your chin. A simple way to remember is: the more formal the wed-ding, the longer the veil. If attached to a hat or cap, the veil should end somewhere above the mouth.

"Why do women wear face (blusher) veils?"

Historically, a face veil was used for arranged marriages. The groom didn't know what the bride looked like until he married her and lifted the veil. Most brides who use blusher veils today just like the custom and choose to follow it. Some religious denominations require brides to wear face veils.

"Am I too old to wear a veil?"

An older bride does not customarily wear a veil. However if you really want to wear one it's not an overwhelming breach of etiquette.

"Would a widow or a divorcée wear a veil?"

Divorcées and widows do not wear veil headpieces unless they are required by their religious traditions.

"When should I wear gloves?"

When required. The only time they must be worn is if your wedding style is very formal.

"How do I know what kind of gloves to wear?"

They should enhance your overall look by blending with the style, fabric, and ornamentation of your gown. If you are wearing a long-sleeved dress, your gloves should end at the wrist. Opera length or gloves covering the entire arm look best with a sleeveless gown.

"How do I manage a ring exchange with gloves?"

You can have just the ring finger slit or wear fingerless gloves.

"What shoe style should I wear?"

It really depends on your gown or dress. If you have a long, sweeping train, wear pumps. With a cocktail or knee-length gown, wear spike heels.

"What material should my wedding shoes be made of? Do my wedding shoes have to be covered with fabric?"

Shoes should match the style and color of your dress. They may be covered with richly ornamented fabrics or topped with satin rosettes, jewels, lace, bows, sequins, or rhinestones.

"What jewelry should I wear?"

Simplicity is the key. The more elaborate your gown, the simpler your jewelry should be. Pearls are a very traditional choice, as is a simple gold locket. Your gown's coloring should also influence your choice. For example, an ivory gown looks best with gold, a bright white dress with pearls, a softer off-white dress with silver, yellow or white gold, or pearls. Some brides like to combine elements of the gown's ornamentation—such as beads, crystals, and seed pearls—into their jewelry.

"Can I wear white if I've been married before?"

Yes. White was once supposed to be indicative of a bride's virginity. Now, it's just the traditional color for the bride's garments. Formal, traditional wedding gowns are usually white, although ivory is also acceptable.

"What is the most traditional and formal fabric for wedding gowns?"

Satin in the winter, taffeta or lace in the spring, chiffon or organdy in the summer, and brocade or velvet in the fall.

"Who accompanies the bride in choosing her gown?"

It's not easy to make the selection alone. Traditionally the bride's mother comes along. If that's not possible, the maid or matron of honor fills that role. Many brides bring both.

Groom Attire

"What would a groom wear to a formal daytime wedding?"

His jacket style might be tailcoat cutaway, stroller, or tuxedo. Trousers would match or contrast the jacket. He'd wear a white shirt with a wing collar and French cuffs. Traditionally the cummerbund and vest match. He can choose to wear an ascot or striped tie. Accessories such as top hats and gloves are optional.

"A formal evening wedding?"

A formal wedding after 6 P.M. is the most elaborate wedding style. A wing-collared shirt, bow tie, and a full-dress tailcoat with matching trousers and waistcoat is the traditional male attire.

"A semiformal daytime wedding?"

The groom would wear a white shirt, four-in-hand tie or ascot, and a gray cutaway coat with matching striped trousers and matching waistcoat; or a tuxedo jacket with matching trousers, a cummerbund or waistcoat, and a plain or pleated front shirt and bow tie.

"A semiformal evening wedding?"

Black or midnight blue tuxedo jacket with matching trousers, a waistcoat or cummerbund, a bow tie, and a plain or pleated front shirt.

Attendant Attire

"How can an out-of-town attendant be measured for their attire?"

Have your attendants visit a formal wear shop in their area and ask to be measured. That formal wear shop will send those measurements to your local formal wear shop.

"Who selects the bridesmaids' dresses?"

Because bridesmaids pay for their own apparel, most brides feel it's fair to give them a voice in the selection. But to avoid too much confusion, visit the shop ahead of time and select three or four dresses that you like. Then allow them to choose among those selections.

"What should my bridesmaids and maid/matron of honor wear?"

For a formal wedding the bridesmaid and maid of honor gowns should be floor length; ankle length is acceptable for a daytime wedding. The gown's color and style should be complementary to the bride's dress. Shoes should blend or match with the gown. Gloves, if the bride wants, should be worn with sleeveless gowns. Jewelry is up to the bride.

For semi-formal, informal, and casual weddings the bridesmaid and maid of honor attire should be similar in style, fabric, and formality to the bride's. In other words, if your gown is a formal, elaborate satin with a two-foot train, you would not select casual, knee-length cotton lace dresses for your attendants.

"How do I choose something they will want to wear?"

It is wise to visit the shop ahead of time and select three or four dresses that you like. Then allow them to choose among those selections. Remember to consider their body types. For example, heavier friends would not look their best in slinky skintight knits.

"Must the bridesmaid's dresses be identical in color?"

Not necessarily. In more formal and traditional weddings, they are dressed identically. Some brides select hues of the same color (such as light blue to dark blue). In less formal celebrations, a bride might select complementary colors such as pale peach, pale yellow, and cream. Sometimes the honor attendant wears a different hue than the bridesmaids.

"What should my junior bridesmaid wear?"

They are part of the wedding party but not adults. If the other attendant's gowns are more sophisticated, choose something that complements their gowns. A similar color, pattern, or fabric would be most appropriate.

"Do I invite my junior bridesmaid to my wedding shower or bachelorette party?"

They would only attend the appropriate wedding activities: rehearsal dinner, wedding ceremony, and reception. You wouldn't include them in a personal shower or bachelorette party.

"May I tell my attendants how to wear their hair or what jewelry to wear?"

You may suggest that they wear a certain type of jewelry or particular hairstyle. However you really can't and shouldn't order them to do so.

"Does the flower girl wear the same headpiece as the bridesmaids?"

It is rarely the same as the rest of the female attendants. Many young girls wear ribbons of the wedding colors trailing from a pretty barrette or a wreath of silk flowers. Some wear nothing on their heads at all.

"Should the groom's attendants wear matching attire?"

Males in the wedding party wear the same style of clothing as the groom. This includes the fathers of the bride and groom. The groom might wear a different tie or cummerbund to distinguish himself from the rest.

"What should the ring bearer wear?"

Usually dressed similarly to the men, but in shorts or knickers instead of trousers. For less formal weddings he can dress in matching colors in dressy children's clothing.

"What if I have chosen a male attendant instead of a bridesmaid or maid of honor?"

If the bride chooses a male attendant, or the groom a female attendant, they would still dress appropriately in the traditional mode of their sex. A female attendant among groomsmen would wear a dress or suit that blended with the rest. A male attendant among bridesmaids would wear a suit or tuxedo that fit the formality of the occasion.

Parent Attire

"What should our fathers wear?"

Fathers should dress to match the men in the wedding party.

"What should our mothers wear?"

Mothers of the bride and groom should be complementary in style with one another. The length and fabric should fit in with the dresses worn by the bride and her attendants. They do need to wear the same color, nor do they need to match the bridesmaids' gowns. Darker colors are acceptable for more formal evening weddings.

Black implies disapproval or mourning when worn by the mother of the bride or groom. Hats and gloves are usually worn only at formal weddings.

Guest Attire

"How will my guests know what to wear?"

Some invitations make it easy by specifying the correct attire, such as "black tie" or "blue jeans." If not, the guest searches for clues in the style of invitation and time of day. If it's on heavy paper with engraved wording, they dress formally. If it's computer-generated they know it will be an informal affair.

"What should guests wear to a formal wedding?"

For a formal day wedding, female guests should wear lighter colors in dressy fabrics. Dresses should be cocktail length or longer. Embroidery, lace, and other ornamentation are acceptable. Jewelry and accessories should be sophisticated, but not too ornate. Men should wear a light-colored suit with a dress shirt, vest, and tie. For a formal evening wedding (after 6 P.M.), women should wear a cocktail length or longer dress in a darker color. Sophisticated fabrics with some beading or sequins are acceptable. Men should wear a dark suit and tie or a tuxedo.

"What does it mean when 'black tie' is specified?"

For women it means wearing a formal floor-length dress with ornate accessories, such as expensive jewelry, beaded purses, and silk or pashmina wraps. For men it means a tuxedo.

"What should guests wear to a semiformal wedding?"

For a daytime wedding, women should wear a dressy skirt and blouse, light-colored suit, or flowing dress at calf or knee length. Men should wear a light-colored suit or a coat and tie with dress slacks. For an evening wedding, women should wear something similar to a day wedding, but in a more sophisticated fabric and style. Think cocktail dress, or the kind of attire you might wear for an expensive dinner or evening at the theater. Men should wear a dark suit or coat and tie with dark dress slacks.

"What should a wedding guest avoid wearing?"

A guest should not dress in a way that draws attention to themselves and away from the bride and groom. Clothes should fit properly and not be too revealing. Consider the location. For example, don't plan to wear high heels to a beach wedding. A strapless dress (unless covered by a jacket or shawl) is often considered inappropriate at a religious ceremony. Dark colors, especially black, are considered wrong for a daytime wedding. It's also a courtesy not to wear white as it takes away from the bride.

Wedding Web Sites

Having a wedding Web site is a handy way to quickly communicate details and information regarding the wedding to attendants, family, and friends. There are countless sites that guide you through creating your own page. You can create a free, simple wedding Web site at www.theknot.com and more elaborate customized ones for a small fee at many online sites. As for content, your site might include:

- Date and times of ceremony and reception
- Maps to the ceremony and reception sites
- Photographs of the happy couple
- Lodging information for out-of-town guests
- Local car rentals, restaurants, and sites to see for out-of-town guests
- Blog entries updating the wedding plans
- Links to gift registries
- An option to RSVP online
- Wedding and honeymoon pictures after the events

"How do I let everyone know about the Web site?"

E-mail the address to those who would be interested. But remember that there are still people who aren't comfortable using computers. Others might have difficulty accessing e-mail. In cases where you aren't sure, mail printed copies of important details such as maps and directions.

"How can I encourage family and friends to RSVP online?"

Add a line at the bottom of your reception reply card. It might say something like:

You have the option of replying electronically if you prefer. Please visit our wedding Web site at www. amyjoemarried.com.

"Should we print the wedding Web site address on the invitation?"

It might be easier to print the address on the invitation, but it would be poor etiquette. The tradition of what information appears on the invitation is a strong one. Unless your wedding is very informal, you should avoid this option.

"How do I add information about gift registries?"

Have a discrete section on your wedding Web site with links to each gift registry location. You want to make finding your gift registry information convenient for your guests, but your home page shouldn't look like a blatant plea for guests to visit the registry.

3

You Are
Invited

The Guest List

"How do we decide how many people to invite?"

That depends on your budget and the style of your wedding. If you can, you should include all the people you would truly miss if they weren't there.

"What percentage of those invited will probably attend?"

Generally 75 percent will attend. The number can be affected by adverse weather, summer vacations, and other activities that may conflict with your wedding date.

"Does the bride's family get to invite more guests?"

No. Although the bride's family traditionally sets the size of the guest list, the groom's family may use half the allotted slots.

"What if one family is larger?"

Traditionally it doesn't matter whose family is larger. If 200 guests will be invited, each side has the option of inviting 100. Often if one side doesn't need enough invitations for half of the guests, they offer those slots to the other side.

"How can I trim the guest list?"

It's easiest to make a rule—for example, no neighbors, third cousins, or coworkers—that applies to both families.

"I've been married before, may I invite the same guests?"

Invite them! If you are still close to them, they will surely rejoice in your second chance at happiness.

"Several acquaintances of mine seem to assume they'll be invited. There really isn't room. Should I explain or just invite them anyway?"

Because weddings are joyful, celebratory events, many people like to attend, but you should not let such assumptions affect your plans. No one has a "right" to an invitation.

"My aunt's neighbor gave us a beautiful gift. I wasn't planning to invite her, but now my aunt says I must. This will only offend other people I'm not able to invite. Should I return the gift?"

No, that would be offensive. Send her a thank-you note for the gift. Explain that you are sorry you cannot extend an invitation to the wedding because the guest list is limited. Suggest having a get-together for lunch or dinner after the wedding.

"Should I invite two aunts who don't speak? I don't want their anger ruining my celebrations."

Invite them both to the shower. If they can't behave, you will then know what might happen on your wedding day.

"My mother says that if my father comes, she is staying home. What should I do?"

It's frustrating when adults act like children, and weddings often bring out emotions and childishness that are otherwise kept hidden. It's your wedding and you shouldn't give in to such emotional blackmail. If your mother would truly stay away from your wedding over such an issue, she doesn't deserve to be there. However in most cases like this, once people realize that emotional blackmail will not work, they abandon their misguided attitudes.

"My fiancé's mother has decided to wear black because she doesn't approve of me. Should we tell her to stay home?"

Too often, what should be a day of celebration turns into a day of emotional banner waving. Let her come. Think how ridiculous she will look in the wedding pictures when you display them at your 25th anniversary party.

"Do we have to allow each single friend to bring a guest?"

No. If someone is engaged or part of a well-established couple, that person's partner should be included. In that case, his or her partner's name would be written out on the envelope as well.

"How far away does someone have to live to be considered an out-of-town guest?"

Generally if they are driving four hours, or about 160 miles away, they are "out of town."

"My guest list keeps growing because both of our mothers keep adding names. How do I stop this?"

This is a common problem with large weddings. Your mother has probably talked about the wedding with the members of her bridge club for the past six months. They feel so much like part of the planning to her that she now wants them to be part of the celebration. Your fiancé's mother may have done the same with her friends at work. The only way to stop it is to talk with each woman and firmly establish a "no more names" rule. No exceptions allowed.

"I'm very close to my 10-year-old niece; I want to invite her to the wedding but not any other children. May I just invite the children I like?"

Only if he or she will be part of the wedding party. Traditionally children in the wedding party and brothers and sisters of the bride and groom are always invited. After that, if you invite one child, you must invite all children of guests.

"My fiancé's daughter is four, and will be the flower girl in our wedding. Must I invite her mother?"

No, but someone trustworthy should be in charge of watching over the daughter during the ceremony and reception.

"Should I send invitations to people when I know they won't be able to attend the wedding? I am afraid they will see it as my hoping for a gift."

Yes, you should still send an invitation. If you don't they will feel left out, which is clearly not your intention. Let them decide if they want to send you a gift. And you never know; they just may be able to attend.

"I don't like my sister's boyfriend. Must I invite him?"

If they are a socially recognized couple, meaning engaged or living together, you must invite him. The fact that he's your sister's boyfriend makes it a bigger potential land mine if you don't.

"Must I invite all relatives who invited me to their weddings?"

No, but you might want to drop them a note explaining that you are having a smaller affair.

"Must I invite all relatives of equal rank if I invite one of them?"

A wedding is a family celebration and the answer depends on the family. In some, if you don't invite them all, it will create hard feelings.

"I haven't spoken to my cousin in eight years. Must I invite a close relative if I'm not speaking to her?"

Deliberately leaving one person out of the picture has potential for creating hurt feelings. Talk to her mother. If her mother understands your feelings, then it's up to you. If she prefers that you invite her, offer the invitation as an olive branch. And if your cousin refuses to come, well, you tried, didn't you?

"I'm a widow, and my children and I have remained very close to his family. I want to invite my first husband's parents and siblings to the wedding. My fiancé doesn't mind, but my mother says it's insulting to my fiancé's family."

Ask your fiancé to talk with his parents to ensure there are no misunderstandings or hard feelings. Having their father's family join the celebration would definitely help your children understand that they are not losing one family, but gaining another. You should also discuss the idea with your first husband's parents. As much as they may wish you joy, it might also be extremely painful for them to watch you marry and recall a previous wedding day.

> *"Several of my bridesmaids are offended because I'm not inviting their parents. Am I supposed to add them to the guest list?"*

Are you related to their parents? Have you known them for many years? In those situations you might be expected to include them. However every guest list has its limits.

Save-the-Date Cards

These are a great way to let everyone know what date to mark on their calendars. There are many forms and styles, from simple notes, refrigerator magnets, and postcards, to brochures and booklets. The most important information to include are:

- ◆ Your names
- ◆ Wedding date
- ◆ Location (city and state)
- ◆ Wedding Web site address (if applicable)
- ◆ "Invitation to follow"

"Must I send one to everyone on my guest list?"

No. However if someone is traveling from out of town, the additional advance notice will increase their chances of being there. This is also true for those with busy schedules. You should, however, plan on sending save-the-date cards to all guests if your wedding will take place during a holiday. The only rule of etiquette: send them to people that will eventually receive a wedding invitation. If you are not planning to invite them, don't ask them to save the date.

"How far ahead of the wedding date should they be sent?"

It depends on the date, location, and type of wedding. Are you marrying during the holidays? Or during summer when many are traveling? Are you planning a destination wedding? The easiest answer is the sooner the better. More specifically, for a destination wedding, 12–15 months before will allow more friends and family to plan ahead. At minimum they should be sent a few months before the actual invitations.

"Can I enclose them with the invitations for my engagement party?"

Yes, that's a great way of letting everyone know the details. Otherwise you may find yourself repeating the date and location over and over to your guests.

Here's an example of wording for the card:

Mark your calendar! Save the date!
Kelly and Jake are getting married on March 1, 2016,
in Louisville, Kentucky.

Invitation to follow.
Visit our wedding Web site: www.kellyjakewedding.com.

Wedding Invitations

"How do I know what kind of invitation to choose for my style of wedding?"

A thick, white, richly engraved invitation announces a very formal wedding. A handwritten note or computer-generated card implies a small, informal gathering.

"Where can I find invitation examples?"

Online, bridal shops, some department stores, florists, photographers, catalogs, and any stores involved in the wedding trade.

"What does a traditional, formal invitation look like?"

It's on thick, quality paper in cream or ivory and has a plain design with, at most, a simple border. Text appears on the front, engraved in thick black ink.

"Are wedding invitations always issued by the bride's parents?"

Traditionally yes, even if they aren't contributing to the expenses.

"Am I too old to have the invitation issued by my parents?"

An older bride (especially one who has been married before) might wish to issue the invitation in her and her fiancé's name, but it's not necessary.

"Who else can issue the invitation?"

If circumstances won't allow the bride's parents to be the hosts, the invitations may be issued by a guardian, a friend, or the bride and groom. Sometimes the groom's parents are included on the invitation, but that's entirely optional.

"Why is there white tissue paper with the invitations?"

Historically it was to keep the ink from the engraving from smearing. Now many follow the custom because they're used to seeing it that way.

"At what age would a child receive his or her own invitation?"

In some cultures and religious denominations, a child of 13 is considered an adult. If your background is different, then children's names would go on the parent's invitation. A separate invitation is sent to those over 16.

"Why do invitations always say the 'honor of your presence'?"

Invitations don't always say it. That's the traditional wording for invitations to the church ceremony.

"What's the traditional way of wording an invitation to the wedding reception?"

The invitation says "request the pleasure of your company."

"If it's a double wedding, which bride's name is first on the invitation?"

The elder bride's name would be first.

"If I'm a doctor, does that designation belong on the invitation?"

Traditionally it appears only if you and your groom are issuing the invitation.

"What kind of doctor must I be to include the doctor designation on the invitation?"

A doctor of medicine or doctor of theology would be designated as doctor. A person with an academic doctorate wouldn't use the title of doctor.

"My father died when I was young. My grandmother insists that his name should be included on the announcement and on the invitation. Is this OK?"

It's understandable that your grandmother wants your father to be a part of your wedding, but only the living can announce something or issue an invitation.

"Do I send invitations to the people in the wedding party? What about the officiant?"

They're also keepsakes of the occasion. Your attendants and the officiant should receive invitations.

"I work in a small company of 28 people. Rather than mail all those invitations, I put one up on the bulletin board inviting everyone to come and celebrate. I have been told that this is rude. Is that true?"

Every invited guest should receive an invitation. If you can't afford to send one to each, then you should cut back on your wedding. Bulletin board invitations are generally considered an invitation to the ceremony only. No gift is expected of someone who attends. At this point, you can explain the misunderstanding to your coworkers. But you can't prove them wrong, because they are not.

"We're planning an informal wedding and I just want to e-mail my invitations. I know all of my guests have e-mail. My future mother-in-law is very upset, is she overreacting?"

Although e-mails, IMs, and text messages are all quicker, they diminish the importance of the occasion. A handwritten note, telephone call, or computer-generated invitation (printed and mailed) are as informal as invitations should be.

Wording on the Invitations

"What is the traditional invitation wording?"

Mr. and Mrs. Nathan Matthew Hunter
request the honor of your presence
at the marriage of their daughter

Mackenzie Alexis
to
Logan Joshua Bailey
on
Saturday, the ninth of August
Two thousand and fourteen
at four o'clock
Congregational Reformed Church
12 East State Street
Providence, Rhode Island

"What is the correct wording for an invitation issued in special circumstances?"

Bride's mother is widowed:

Mrs. Jacob Connor
requests the honor of your presence
at the marriage of her daughter
Olivia Faith Connor
to
Cody Parker Cusick
on
Saturday, the third of November
Two thousand and fifteen
at one o'clock
Holy Family Catholic Church
841 New Mountain Highway
Palos Heights, Wyoming

Bride's parents are both divorced and remarried; invitation is issued by her parents alone:

Mrs. Aaron Samuel Sheppard
and
Mr. Michael Paul Maldanado
request the pleasure of your company
at the marriage of their daughter
Alanna Grace Maldanado
to
Mason Anthony Peitrellio
on
Friday, the first of February
Two thousand and fourteen
at four o'clock
Farmington Hills Opera House
923 Pavilion Road
Rivertown, Ohio

Bride's parents are both divorced and remarried; invitation is issued to include stepparents:

Mr. and Mrs. Austin Garret Larierre
and
Mr. and Mrs. Brendan Jared Mackenzie
request the pleasure of your company
at the marriage of their daughter
Gabriella Claire Mackenzie
to
Dylan Chase Hayden

on
Saturday, the eighth of May
Two thousand and fourteen
at eleven o'clock
First Congregational Church
1001 Moran Street
Bridgeman, Connecticut

Bride's stepmother and father issue the invitation:

Mr. and Mrs. Adam Ngyun
request the honor of your presence
at the marriage of Mrs. Ngyun's stepdaughter
Jadyn Alexandra
to
Kao Nayimoto
on
Sunday, the seventh of June
Two thousand and fourteen
at two thirty in the afternoon
Wildwood Lake Park
Rogers Road
Sausalito, California

Both the bride's and the groom's parents issue the invitation:

Mr. and Mrs. Joshua Paige Dolenz
request the honor of your presence
at the marriage of their daughter
Erin Victoria
to
Mr. Lucas Ian Sabato
son of Mr. and Mrs. Jackson Lucas Sabato
on
Monday, the fourth of July
Two thousand and sixteen
at four o'clock
Crooked Tree Country Club
1189 Bluehill Drive
Bennington, Kentucky

The groom's parents issue the invitation:

Mr. and Mrs. Noah Henry Herrera
request the honor of your presence
at the marriage of
Annalise Joy Vasquez
to their son
Mr. Wyatt Dominick Herrera
on
Saturday, the twelfth of August
Two thousand and sixteen
at five thirty in the afternoon
St. James Episcopal Church
9547 Cecily Road
Houston, Texas

The bride and groom issue the invitation:

The honor of your presence
is requested at the marriage of
Miss Chloe Alyssa Payton
to
Mr. Aiden Connor Kelorchak
on
Saturday, the first of September
Two thousand and fifteen
at four o'clock
Violet Grace Gardens
821 Lakeshore Drive
Poulsbo, Washington

The bride and groom issue the invitation; bride is a doctor:

The honor of your presence
is requested
at the marriage of
Dr. Lauren Charlotte Landsdon
to
Mr. Colton Carter Gage
Sunday, the eleventh of May
Two thousand and fifteen
at six o'clock in the evening
First Presbyterian Church
53 Chestnut Drive
Baytown, Massachusetts

The bride's parents issue the invitation; bride's mother is a doctor:

> Dr. Anna Moses and Mr. Allen Fitz
> request the honor of your presence
> at the marriage of their daughter
> Adrienne Aurora Fitz
> to
> Mr. Zachary Thomas Green
> Friday, the twenty-fifth of June
> Two thousand and eighteen
> at half past six o'clock
> Our Savior Lutheran Church
> 5224 Magnolia Street
> Newport, Rhode Island

Double wedding invitation where the brides are not sisters:

> Mr. and Mrs. Duncan Kyle Herrickson
> and
> Mr. and Mrs. Francisco Renaldo Tubalo
> request the honor of your presence
> at the marriage of their daughters
> Savannah Skye Herrickson
> to
> Mr. Oliver Nym Lucetta
> and
> Beatrice Amelia Tubalo
> to
> Mr. Tyrese Kendall Ortiz
> Saturday, the tenth of August

> Two thousand and seventeen
> at half past five o'clock
> Hyatt Regency Hotel
> 12422 Highway 11 South
> Grand Forks, North Dakota

Double wedding invitation of sisters:

> Mr. and Mrs. Jared Elliot Grazionce
> request the honor of your presence
> at the marriage of their daughters
> Chloe Annabelle
> to
> Mr. Jacob Asher Seymour
> and
> Rachel Catherine
> to
> Mr. Joseph Michael Lamothe
> Saturday, the eleventh of April
> Two thousand and seventeen
> at half past four o'clock
> United Methodist Church
> 8214 Old Turtle Creek Boulevard
> Sante Fe, New Mexico

Wedding ceremony and reception on one invitation:

> Mr. and Mrs. Gavin John Willison
> request the honor of your presence
> at the marriage of their daughter
> Emma Abigail
> to
> Mr. Bryce Joseph Cameron
> Saturday, the sixth of July
> Two thousand and fourteen
> at half after seven o'clock
> United Methodist Church
> Seventh and Main Streets
> and afterward at the reception
> Willow Hills Country Club
> 350 Forest Hill Lane
> The favor of a reply is requested
> 2323 Vine Lane
> Pittsburgh, Pennsylvania

Small, informal wedding:

> Dear Liam and Sadie,
> Brianna and Logan will be married at 8 P.M. on Friday, April
> 16, at Marquette Park. A small reception will follow.
> Please join us for this happy occasion.
> Love,
> Amanda and Christopher

"How would military titles be noted on the invitations?"

For higher ranks in the Army, Navy, and Reserves, the title appears on the same line, before the name. For the Army that is the rank of Captain or above, and in the Navy, the rank of lieutenant senior grade or above. For example:

Major Aleain Shale Johnson
United States Army

Lieutenant Colonel Jeremy Michael Jeeves
United States Naval Reserve

For lower ranks, the title is listed after the name.

Kelly Ann Pearson
Ensign, United States Navy

Enclosure Cards

"Do I need to enclose a reception card with my invitation?"

Guests today expect to be invited to both the ceremony and reception. In many cases, the information is included on the same invitation as the ceremony. The primary exception would be for very formal weddings, which follow tradition much more closely.

"What is the traditional reception card wording?"

The card is issued by the same party that issues the wedding invitations. For example:

> Mr. and Mrs. Donavin Lane Pettit
> request the pleasure of your company
> on Saturday, the third of August
> Two thousand and fifteen
> at half after six o'clock in the evening
> Bay Harbor Yacht Club
> 11 Lakeshore Road
> Portland, Maine

"How would I add reception information to the ceremony invitation?"

Place the information in the bottom left-hand corner. If they will take place at the same location, it might read:

Reception following the ceremony

If the reception will be at a different location it might read:

Reception at six o'clock
Lake Timberland Pavilion
19 Kingsridge Drive
Wendalla, Oregon

Receptions for adults only:

The pleasure of your company is requested
at a reception for adults

at four thirty in the evening
Monroe Pavilion
759 Remington Drive
Helena, Montana

"Should I send response or RSVP cards? I think they make it easy for guests to inform you if they're coming. However etiquette books say that these shouldn't be included. Why?"

In theory everyone who you invite should know that they are expected to make a written response to your invitation as soon as possible. Most etiquette experts consider it insulting to your guests to do the work for them by including a response card. In reality, these cards have become customary in many regions and guests rely on them to respond. You should request for their response to arrive three weeks before your wedding date.

"I have a wedding Web site and want to offer the option of responding electronically. How do I notify the guests?"

Add a note at the bottom of the response card, such as, "You have the option of replying electronically if you prefer. Please visit our wedding Web site: www.amyjoemarried.com."

"I want to include a card that lists where we are registered to make it convenient for my guests. Why is it considered wrong in the world of etiquette?"

Because it's rude to seem to expect gifts. If your guest wants to know where you are registered, they will ask.

Addressing Envelopes

"Why shouldn't I address my invitations through my computer? My mother insists that they be addressed by hand. Why?"

Historically invitations were addressed by hand because there was no other option. The practice has continued because it offers a personal touch. Also, only blue or black ink is used. Preprinted labels are associated with junk mail and are not considered suitable for an occasion as dignified as a wedding.

"How do I address the inner and outer envelopes?"

The inner envelope lists those actually invited to the wedding. Traditionally if a person's name isn't on it, he or she isn't invited. On both envelopes, all names are completely written out. No abbreviations are used.

"Where do I write the return address on the outer envelope?"

On the back flap.

"What if I don't want children to attend?"

Don't write their names on the inner envelope.

"What if I'm addressing to a married couple?"

Outer envelope would read their full married names without abbreviation—Mr. and Mrs. Frederick Paul Rodgers.

Inner envelope would read—Mr. and Mrs. Rodgers.

"What if I am addressing to a married couple and the wife has kept her maiden name?"

Outer envelope would list both full names, alphabetically—
Ms. Rhonda Joan Kellerman
Mr. Joshua Ashford St. Clair

Inner envelope would read—
Ms. Kellerman
Mr. St. Clair

"How do I address an envelope for a single person and his or her guest?"

Learn the guest's name and include it on the envelope. You shouldn't write "and Guest" because a wedding isn't the same as a concert ticket. A person participating in your celebration should be someone you know. If a friend is bringing a date, you should at least know the date's name.

"How do I politely address for a single person and no guest?"

Simply write that person's name on the envelope. Don't add anything else.

Assembling and Mailing Invitations

"What is the traditional way to assemble the invitations?"

Place any enclosure cards and maps inside the invitation. Put the invitation in the inner envelope fold-side down. The print side faces the back flap. Don't seal the inner envelope. Place the inner envelope inside the outer envelope. The front side, where the names are written, should face the outer envelope's back flap. Seal the outer envelope.

"When should I mail invitations?"

Six to eight weeks before your wedding date.

"May I use e-mail invitations?"

This isn't an option if your wedding style is formal. Part of the formality is following tradition.

There's no doubt that the cost of paper invitations, postage, and the time involved in selecting and addressing them can take a bite out of any wedding budget. For an informal or casual wedding, an e-mail invitation supplemented by a wedding Web site can provide quick access to information such as maps, accommodations, and other important details. But you need to ask yourself the following:

- ◆ Can I obtain accurate e-mail addresses for those on my guest list?

- Am I sure that they check their e-mail on a regular basis?
- Am I confident that an invitation sent that way won't take away from the importance of the occasion?
- Will I have an accurate and up-to-date wedding Web page for them to obtain, download, and print necessary information?
- Do I have an alternative plan for older relatives that might feel uncomfortable using this method?
- Will I later regret not having a more substantive souvenir of the occasion?

Many people would still consider this type of invitation to be tacky and in poor taste. Weddings are traditional affairs and major changes are not accepted quickly. Ultimately it's your decision—based on the style of your wedding and the guests you'll be inviting to share your day.

4

Who Does What? And When?

Wedding Timetable

Here is a helpful and ideal timetable. It won't go this smoothly, but these are worthy goals.

You're Engaged!

- Choose your engagement ring.
- Set a wedding date and time.
- Ask people to be your attendants and to join your wedding party.
- Begin to prepare the guest list and ask the groom to do the same.
- Compile information about service providers.
- Reserve the reception site.
- Select the location for the ceremony.
- Choose and meet with the person performing the ceremony (officiant).
- If you are having a religious ceremony, learn what pre-marital counseling may be required.

Ten Months Before . . .

- Book florist, caterer, photographer, videographer, and DJ or musicians
- Consider purchasing wedding insurance.
- Contract for any rental items if they aren't handled by the caterer.
- Discuss possible honeymoon destinations.

Eight Months Before . . .

- Choose your attendants' (both bride and groom) attire.
- Finalize guest list.
- Order invitations, announcements, and other stationary.
- Select your wedding gown and headpiece.
- Choose and order wedding cake.

Five Months Before . . .

- Send out save-the-date cards to future guests.
- Address invitations and announcements.
- Investigate marriage license requirements (waiting periods, required medical tests, etc.).
- Verify that all attendants have been measured for their clothing.
- Investigate accommodations for out-of-town guests.

Three Months Before . . .

- Purchase wedding rings.
- Shop for gifts for attendants, parents, and one another.
- Confer with your officiant about ceremony details.
- Reserve room blocks for out-of-town guests.
- Make appointments for any physical exams and medical tests.
- Book hair stylist and makeup artist.
- Finalize honeymoon plans.
- Finalize and verify details with all service providers.

Two Months Before . . .

- Mail the invitations.
- Design wedding program.

- Obtain accessory items such as a purse, shoes, the ring bearer's pillow, goblets, candles, a guest book, a cake knife, and a garter.
- Plan the bridesmaids' luncheon.
- Organize transportation for bride, groom, and wedding party.

Six Weeks Before . . .

- Discuss ideas and details with the photographer and videographer.
- Formulate the final menu decisions.
- Have your formal bridal portrait done.
- Pick up your gown.
- Verify that all male and female attendants have been fitted for their formal wear.
- Keep records of gifts as they arrive.
- Write thank-you notes immediately upon receiving gifts.
- Finalize time and date of rehearsal and inform attendants and parents.

Four Weeks Before . . .

- Address formal announcements.
- Provide the DJ and/or musicians with a list of your musical selections.
- Advise wedding party of location and estimated time of rehearsal dinner.
- Make a seating chart for the reception.
- Write place cards.
- Confirm that transportation arrangements have been made for all attendants and out-of-town guests on the wedding day.

Two Weeks Before . . .

+ Ask your honor attendant (or mom) to contact guests who haven't responded to invitation.
+ Arrange for someone to say grace before dinner.
+ Complete any required blood and medical tests.
+ Confirm accommodations for out-of-town guests.
+ Have your bridesmaids' luncheon.
+ Obtain the marriage license (or refer to local regulations).
+ Preaddress envelopes for thank-you notes to guests.
+ Prepare a wedding announcement for the newspaper.

One Week Before . . .

+ Confirm details with all professional service providers.
+ Give the final guest count for the reception meal to your caterer.
+ Make a list of names and their pronunciation for the best man to mention in his introduction.
+ Make sure that the marriage license has been picked up.
+ Pick up your wedding rings.
+ Make sure programs are printed and ready.
+ Finalize seating chart.
+ Prepare a ceremony seating list for ushers (if necessary).
+ Present the attendants with their gifts.
+ Verify that all of the attendants have picked up and tried on their attire.

One or Two Days Before the Wedding . . .

+ Attend the wedding rehearsal and the rehearsal dinner.
+ Inventory everything you will need for the wedding day and make sure you have it handy.

- Distribute the attendants' gifts if you haven't already done so.
- Review any special ceremony seating arrangements with ushers.
- Tell attendants to arrive at your home about one hour before you'll leave for the ceremony site if you'll be having pictures taken there.
- Do something that helps you relax.

Wedding Day

- Allow yourself plenty of time to get ready.
- Leave early for the ceremony site.
- Try to stay calm.

You're Married!

- Leave for your honeymoon.
- Mail announcements.

One Month After the Wedding . . .

- By now you should have all of your thank-you notes written and mailed.

Financial Responsibilities

"Who pays for what?"

Traditionally the bride's parents paid most of the wedding expenses. Today the financial arrangements are more flexible. The bride's parents are not always willing or able to pay for a large wedding. If the bride is older, she and the groom are expected to pay most, if not all, of the expenses. In fact many couples pay for the entire affair themselves. Others fund it through a combination of contributors including both sets of parents and relatives on both sides of the family.

"What is a sponsor? How many sponsors should I have?"

Customs and traditions have relaxed in the past generation. Where once the wedding bills were entirely the responsibility of the bride's family, it's now acceptable for others to assist in paying for the wedding. A sponsor is somebody who provides financial assistance. Unfortunately, the concept of having sponsors has occasionally been twisted into taking pledges and begging contributions from friends, family, coworkers, and neighbors to help defray the cost of the celebration. Asking for money for any wedding or marriage-related item from anyone except the bride's parents is rude. You may accept money, but you may never ask or hint for it.

"How do I ask my rich relative to help pay for the wedding?"

You don't. Such contributions must be entirely voluntary.

"What if my parents refuse to pay for the wedding I want?"

Having an expensive wedding is not an entitlement you were born with. You should never try to have a wedding that costs more than your contributors can comfortably afford. You should pay the remainder of the cost yourself or trim down your expenses.

"If my parents can't or won't pay for the wedding,
shouldn't I leave their name off the invitation?"

The tradition of placing the bride's parents as hosts of the wedding is not based on financial contributions. Issuing the invitation in their name is traditional, as the bride's mother is automatically considered the hostess. Financial contributions should have nothing to do with it.

"My parents are paying for most of the wedding costs, so
I feel we should honor their wishes. My fiancé says the
final decisions should be ours. Who has the final say in
a decision if my parents are paying the bill?"

This is your special day, and you should both feel comfortable at your own ceremony and reception. Control over the wedding plans is generally based on tradition, not on who contributes the most money. Thus the bride and groom, and then the bride's parents, have the greatest say in the decisions.

"What if my fiancé's parents offer to contribute and my
parents are insulted?"

Many families are now joining together to pay the wedding expenses. Although the bride's family should never ask for assistance, if the groom's family offers, there's no reason to refuse. It isn't necessarily a reflection of their economic status. It's more an outlook of "we're all in this together, so let's pay for it together." But if your parents continue to feel uncomfortable, there's no point in forcing the issue.

"If my fiancé's parents contribute financially, should their names appear on the invitations as cohosts?"

In many cases they are included, whether or not they contribute financially. Their financial contributions do not obligate the bride's family to list them as cohosts, but it would certainly be a nice gesture.

"May we hold a benefit dinner to raise money for our wedding?"

No, that would be rude. The purpose of a wedding is to invite others to share your happiness on the joyful day of joining your lives together. It's not necessary to shake down your friends to make sure that you have the biggest, most expensive party.

"If we are just having a small restaurant dinner after our ceremony, may we ask our guests to pay?"

No. A wedding is a special occasion. You pay the bill for anyone you invite to celebrate with you.

"A bridesmaid has suddenly dropped out. May I make her pay for the deposit on the groomsman's tuxedo that she was supposed to stand with?"

Agreeing to be a bridesmaid doesn't incur any financial obligations toward anyone else in the wedding party. Abandoning her commitment was wrong, but that doesn't mean the groomsman has to drop out. There's no rule that there has to be an equal number of bridesmaids and groomsmen. Let him continue to enjoy being part of the wedding party.

"Who traditionally pays for what?"

Bride pays for:

- Groom's wedding ring
- Any physical examination and medical tests required
- A luncheon for the female attendants and gifts for them
- Lodging for out-of-town attendants

Groom pays for:

- Bride's engagement and wedding rings
- The marriage license
- The cost of any examinations and medical tests required for him
- Bride's bouquet and going-away corsage, as well as flowers for his mother and the mother of the bride, himself, male attendants, and honored male guests
- Gifts for the male attendants
- Lodging for out-of-town attendants
- Wedding officiant's fee

Bride's parents pay for:

- Wedding invitations and announcements (including postage and any other related fees)
- Bride's wedding gown, headpiece, and accessories
- Rental fee for the ceremony and reception sites
- Floral arrangements and decorations for the ceremony and reception sites, and flowers for female attendants and honored female guests
- Costs for food, beverages, catering, and wedding cake

• Photographer, videographer, musicians, security, and transportation expenses

Groom's parents pay for:

• Their own lodging and travel expenses
• The rehearsal dinner
• Any other expenses they would like to assume

Attendants pay for:

• Their own transportation and travel expenses
• Their clothing and accessories
• Gifts for the happy couple

Flower girl and ring bearer's parents pay for:

• Children's clothing and accessories

Guests pay for:

• Their clothing, lodging, and transportation
• Gifts for the bride and groom

Wedding Responsibilities

The bride's parents are the traditional host and hostess of the celebration. They are involved in the planning, although the bride and groom should always have the final word.

"Do the bride's parents have any special responsibilities?"

It's customary for the bride's mother to choose her gown first and then inform the groom's mother of the style and color. At the wedding ceremony, the bride's mother is the last person seated before the ceremony begins, if she isn't part of the processional. The father of the bride typically walks her down the aisle. The bride's mother stands at the head of the receiving line at the reception to greet and introduce the guests. The bride's father isn't required to stand in the receiving line. Some fathers do, others prefer to circulate among the guests.

"Do the groom's parents have any special responsibilities?"

After the engagement announcement, they should contact the bride's family to welcome their daughter to their family. When the bride's mother informs her of her attire, the groom's mother should choose something in similar style, length, and complementary (but different) color. The night before the ceremony, they host a rehearsal dinner for the wedding party and out-of-town guests. The groom's mother stands next to the bride's mother in the receiving line. His father may stand in the line or circulate with guests, whichever he prefers.

"What are the special responsibilities of my maid/matron of honor?"

She assists the bride in selecting the wedding gown and attire for the bridesmaids. She helps address invitations and announcements and helps with writing place cards. She attends the engagement party, usually hosts a wedding or bridal shower, and attends the rehearsal, rehearsal dinner, ceremony, and reception. In the receiving line she stands to the left of the groom. She coordinates with the other attendants, making sure they are at the rehearsal and ceremony on time. Her most important responsibility is to care for the bride throughout the wedding day, including:

- Assisting the bride in dressing
- Making sure hair and makeup are picture perfect
- Keeping the veil and train properly arranged
- Holding the bride's bouquet when necessary
- Holding the groom's ring during the ceremony
- Keeping the bride on schedule
- Signing as a witness on the marriage certificate

"May I fire my maid of honor? She has been a big disappointment; she doesn't seem to know what she is supposed to do. How do I politely tell her?"

Copy the list of duties in this section and pass it along without comment. She should get the picture. If she doesn't, you might ask a mutual friend to talk to her about some of the tasks she needs to accomplish. It's very difficult to fire any wedding attendant, especially an honor attendant, without permanently damaging your relationship.

"What do bridesmaids do?"

They assist the bride and maid/matron of honor by running errands, helping to address invitations and announcements, and fulfilling other reasonable requests related to the wedding. They attend the engagement party and usually assist with any wedding or bridal showers. They are present at the rehearsal and rehearsal dinner, ceremony, and reception. They stand in the receiving line at the bride's discretion.

On the wedding day, their duties include:

- Taking part in the processional and recessional
- Posing for pictures
- Providing backup support as needed
- Helping with elderly or disabled guests
- Assisting in gathering guests for special moments (such as cake cutting)
- Dance with ushers and groomsmen if there is dancing at the reception

"What does the best man do?"

He assists the groom in handling all arrangements and details of the wedding. He is present at the engagement party, wedding shower (if invited), rehearsal and rehearsal dinner, ceremony, and reception. He organizes the bachelor party or any pre-wedding party for the groom.

His most important duty is to care for the groom throughout the wedding day, including:

- Helping the groom dress
- Keeping him on schedule
- Reminding him to bring the ring and marriage certificate

- Standing at the groom's side during the ceremony
- Holding the bride's ring during the ceremony
- Walking in the recessional
- Offering introductions and first toast to the new couple at the reception
- Dancing with the bride, maid/matron of honor, bridesmaids, and mothers
- Delivering tips, fees, or payments to the officiant, musicians, and others as prearranged
- Signing as a witness on the marriage certificate

"What do the groomsmen and ushers do?"

The role is often combined. If not, ushers have duties prior to the ceremony while groomsmen do not. The groomsmen assist the groom throughout the wedding, including:

- Attending any parties for the groom, the rehearsal and rehearsal dinner, ceremony, and reception
- Passing out programs prior to the ceremony
- Assisting in seating guests
- Placing the aisle runner after the guests are seated
- Walking in the processional and recessional
- Posing for wedding pictures
- Providing backup support as needed, help with elderly or disabled guests
- Inviting guests to sign the guest book
- Dancing with the bride, maid/matron of honor, bridesmaids, and mothers of the bride and groom

5
The Wedding Ceremony

First Decisions

"We're both of the same denomination. Whose church do we marry in?"

Traditionally the marriage takes place in the bride's church. If for some reason that's a problem or source of contention, perhaps an alternative third site would be an acceptable compromise.

"We're of different denominations. How do we choose which church to marry in?"

Select the one you both feel most comfortable with. Or you may compromise with a nondenominational church or civil ceremony.

"We're getting married in a religious denomination different from our families. How do I advise them about an unfamiliar service?"

The general rule is to follow the lead of the congregation. Stand, sit, sing, and pray when everyone else does. If there's a part that they don't wish to participate in, they should sit quietly until that portion of the service is over. For example, Protestants in a Catholic church are not expected to genuflect, cross themselves, or kneel. You might also consider printing simple programs for your guests to guide them through the service.

Selecting the Officiant

For some couples, it's important that the officiant is someone that they know and like. For others, anyone qualified can fill the role.

Religious Wedding

Most denominations have specific policies about who may officiate at their location. If you are having a religious ceremony, you must research their rules before selecting the officiant.

Nonreligious Wedding

The ability to perform wedding ceremonies varies, so research the regulations in your area. There are many who advertise their availability and usually focus on a particular group or lifestyle. Or you might choose a civil servant empowered to marry—whether justice of the peace, judge, or mayor. A nondenominational minister can also fill the role.

"Is it rude to ask the officiant how much he or she charges?"

No. It will probably be a relief to the officiant, because he or she will expect to be paid, but it's often an awkward subject to introduce. However, many like to refer to the charge as a donation rather than a fee.

"My uncle is a clergyman. Our local minister has agreed to let him hold the ceremony at our church. Whom do we pay?"

You would give the same donation to your local minister that you would have given him or her if they had performed the ceremony. A personal gift would be more appropriate for your uncle.

Rehearsal

"Why do we need a rehearsal?"

Everyone will be a bit anxious about their role in the ceremony. Your officiant can help ease some of this anxiety by running through duties and answering questions. In addition, practice makes perfect!

"Who schedules it?"

You or your fiancé should. It's not automatically set for the night before the wedding, just traditionally. Be sure to discuss the rehearsal and date with your officiant.

"Must everyone in the wedding party attend?"

If at all possible, yes. Sometimes extenuating circumstances make it unavoidable for a bridesmaid or usher not to be there. If that happens be sure to run through their roles with them before the ceremony.

"Should our parents attend?"

Yes. They should be there if at all possible.

"Our photographer wants to attend. Should we let her?"

Chances are your photographer is just interested in getting a general feel for the next day's activities. Unless your officiant objects, there's no reason she should not be there.

Rehearsal Dinner

"Who hosts the rehearsal dinner?"

The groom's family traditionally hosts the dinner. It's their way of thanking the bride's family for providing for the wedding.

"Must the dinner be formal?"

Not at all. This is supposed to be a relaxing get-together the night before the more formal affair. Anything from a pizza party to a sit-down four-course meal is acceptable. It's all based on what the groom's parents can provide and the bride and groom prefer.

"Whom should we invite?"

Invite the entire wedding party and their significant others; parents and siblings of the bride and groom; child attendants and their parents; and, if you like, the officiant and his or her spouse. It's nice to include guests who have traveled a long way, and in some areas they expect an invitation.

"When can attendants bring dates?"

If they are married, officially engaged, or who have been in a long-term live-in relationship. For anyone else, it's the decision of the groom's parents whether they want to incur the additional financial obligation. You, as the bride, can give your opinion one way or another, but they are the official hosts.

"Should we send invitations?"

It's not necessary to put anything in writing because this is usually a small, informal affair. In most cases guests are notified by phone. However an informal written or printed invitation can be sent. Here is a suggestion for the wording:

> Please join us for the rehearsal dinner
> for the wedding of Liandra and Anthony
> at
> Falling Waters Country Inn
> 113 State Road 59
> on Thursday, September 20
> immediately following
> the wedding rehearsal
> (approximately 8:00 P.M.)
> Mr. and Mrs. Kevin David Van Dyke

"Should we predetermine the menu?"

The wise host would set the menu to avoid an astronomical bill.

"May we ask our guests to pay for their own alcoholic beverages?"

Absolutely not. It's not very nice to invite people for dinner and then ask them to pay for their refreshments.

"Are there any special traditions to observe during the dinner?"

The groom's parents welcome the guests, and then the groom's father makes the first toast. He should express happiness at his son's marriage. The bride's father offers a toast expressing happiness at his daughter's marriage. Usually everyone in the wedding party offers a toast. There are many anecdotes and jokes shared about the happy couple. Sometimes a few creative friends compose a humorous poem or song. Also the bride and groom often distribute gifts to their attendants on this occasion.

Before the Ceremony

"How can we politely ask people to leave their children at home for the ceremony?"

If you insist on this, parents will have the choice of either hiring a babysitter or staying home. Most parents of children who wouldn't be able to behave during a service will leave them home if they can. On the other hand, one of the purposes of marriage is joining two families, and children are a part of the families. A restless child or giggling toddler may not destroy your service; it may just make it more real, more human. However, if you can't abide the idea, then a handwritten note enclosed with the invitation explaining your reasons would be the best way to avoid offense. Be sure to mention that no children will be invited, otherwise they may feel that you are singling out their little darlings!

"How can we inform our guests that they should not take photographs during the ceremony? Is there a gentle way to remind them to turn off their cell phones too?"

A sign in the vestibule, a note on the ceremony program, or a brief announcement from the head usher before the mothers of the bride and groom are seated would all be satisfactory options.

"If I spot an uninvited guest before the ceremony, what should I do?"

Is your ceremony in a location with limited seating? Are you a celebrity, or is there some other reason you need to control access to the site? If so, then you would definitely ask the ushers to quietly escort them out. However, if they're sitting in the back quietly and not taking the space of an invited guest, you may just leave them there if you like.

"What if a guest arrives late to the ceremony?"

If the mother of the bride has already been seated, the guest should quietly sit in an empty pew behind the other guests. If the wedding party has already begun to walk down the aisle, they should stay outside the sanctuary until the bride has taken her place at the altar.

Wedding Programs

These are a guide to the wedding ceremony. They're especially helpful if you're having an interfaith or intercultural marriage, so that guests will understand all that is happening. In any case, having the words to prayers and hymns will help guests follow and participate. They're also a souvenir if you have written your own vows.

"What should a program look like?"

Depending on your budget and the formality of the ceremony, it can be as simple as a single printed sheet to as elaborate as an engraved program. Many couples design a cover and program on their personal computers. If your ceremony site is especially attractive, you might include a photo or sketch of it on your cover.

"What information should I include in the program?"

Most wedding programs contain the following:

+ Date, time, and place
+ Full names of bride, groom, their parents, the officiant, attendants, soloists, and musicians
+ Titles of readings and songs played
+ Any explanations of customs you feel will be helpful
+ Your wedding vows
+ Thank you to guests and parents
+ Any special information about ceremony site
+ Information about or map for getting to reception site

"Who pays for the programs?"

The bride's family; programs are part of the wedding stationery.

Who Sits Where?

"How do you know which is the bride or groom's 'side'?"

In Christian denominations, the bride's family is seated on the left, the groom's on the right. The opposite is true for Jewish weddings and some military weddings.

Bride's Mother

She is seated by the head usher, in the aisle seat of the first row behind the attendants. If she is not part of the processional, she is seated just before the ceremony is about to begin.

Bride's Father

After the bride's father escorts the bride in the processional, he joins the bride's mother in the first row after the attendants.

Groom's Parents

They are seated in the aisle seats of the first row behind the attendants. If they are not taking part in the processional, the groom's mother is seated by the head usher about five minutes before the ceremony begins; the groom's father follows behind.

Children of the Bride or Groom

They sit in the row behind the attendants.

"What if our parents are divorced?"

The problem with having a traditional wedding in a nontraditional world is there aren't always easy answers. Here are suggestions on how to handle the most common situations:

Neither Parents Remarried, on Friendly Terms

Divorced parents are usually separated in seating arrangements due to animosity. If there is none, there's no reason they shouldn't sit together in their traditional places.

Both Parents Remarried

The bride's mother would sit on the aisle in the row behind the attendants with her current spouse. The bride's father would sit on the aisle with his wife in the row just behind the bride's mother.

Bride Raised by Father, Not Mother

The first row behind the attendants should go to the person who mostly raised you. Traditionally it is the mother, but if the father was the one to raise you, then he would sit in that row. In cases where it's a difficult call, sometimes flipping a coin or drawing straws is the only way.

Boyfriend or Girlfriend of Bride's Parent

There's no reason etiquettewise that they shouldn't be seated with the parent.

Stepchildren of Bride's Parents

Unless they are especially close to the bride or groom, they should sit farther back—third or fourth row in most cases.

Grandparents

If the family is small, there's no reason they can't sit in the first row behind the attendants. They and other close relatives sit in the same row as or behind siblings.

Siblings

Depending on family size, they might sit in the row behind the attendants — or the row after that. If the bride or groom has children, they would sit in the same row as or behind the children.

Seating for a Double Wedding

"My sister and I may have a double wedding. How are two sets of groom's parents seated?"

They may either share the first row or sit one row behind the other. As far as determining who sits in which row or who sits on the aisle seat if they share a row, they can decide the method. Flipping a coin, drawing straws, or any other problem-resolving method they can agree upon might be used.

"My cousin and I are thinking of having a double wedding. Suddenly our mothers are arguing over who will sit on the aisle in the first row. How would we seat our parents?"

They would either share the first row or one would sit in the row behind the other. If they share a row, the elder traditionally sits on the aisle. If they choose to sit one behind the other, they can either allow the elder the row in front or resolve it with a game of chance, such as flipping a coin.

Usher's Role

"What does a head usher do at the ceremony?"

He is chosen by the groom and responsible for coordinating the other ushers in seating the guests. He is aware of which guests should be seated in the honor or reserved section and relays this information to the other ushers.

"Where does the usher seat the guests?"

Ushers stand to the left of the inside door. As guests arrive, the usher asks if they are with the bride or groom and seats them accordingly. In Christian denominations, the bride's family is seated on the left, the groom's on the right. The opposite is true for Jewish weddings and some military weddings.

"How does an usher seat a woman?"

When an usher is seating a woman guest, she takes his arm. Any male accompanying her walks beside the usher. The usher leads the way to a vacant seat and then stands aside while the guest(s) step in. Some early arrivals ask to be seated in choice aisle seats. Unlike the etiquette for normal services, at a wedding they should be allowed to keep their seats on the aisle and not have to move over for new arrivals.

"Does the usher take the arm of a male guest?"

No. He offers his arm to a female guest but merely escorts a male guest. The only exception would be if the guest was quite elderly or having difficulty walking.

"What if two women arrive at the same time and there is only one usher? Whom does the usher seat first?"

The usher should offer his arm to the elder. The other lady may either follow behind or wait for another usher to seat her.

"Would the usher escort a twelve-year-old to their seat?"

Children under the age of fifteen usually follow their parents unescorted.

"What should the ushers do after the bride's mother is seated?"

The aisle carpet is laid and the outer church doors are closed. No one else is formally seated after the bride's mother. Late-arriving guests are asked to stand in the vestibule until the processional is over. They would then seat themselves in the back of the church.

"My family is much larger; won't the seating look out of balance?"

A perfect balance isn't necessary, but in a situation where you know there will be a major imbalance you may have ushers seat guests to balance the sides. The only "rule" is that immediate family should still sit on their traditional side.

"What should the ushers do after the recessional?"

They "bow out" or make a wave or bowing motion to each row of remaining guests, beginning in the front, letting them know it is their time to file out.

Processional and Recessional

The processional is the march of the wedding party into the ceremony site as the ceremony is about to begin. The recessional is their march out.

"What is the proper order for the processional?"

Your ceremony officiant is most likely aware of the customary traditions for your type of wedding. You can discuss it with him or her ahead of time. This is the reason for a rehearsal before the wedding: so everyone knows where he or she will be on the big day. Here are just two of the traditional arrangements. There are many variations:

Christian

1. Groomsmen
2. Bridesmaids
3. Attendants
4. Ring bearer
5. Flower girl
6. Bride and her father

Jewish

1. Cantor
2. Rabbi
3. Bride's grandparents
4. Groom's grandparents
5. Groomsmen
6. Best man
7. Groom, between his father and mother
8. Bridesmaids
9. Maid or matron of honor
10. Ring bearer
11. Flower girl
12. Bride, between her father and mother

"How does the groom enter?"

In Protestant, Catholic, and nondenominational ceremonies, the groom and his honor attendant enter at the front of the church, usually from a side sacristy door. They stand together and await the processional to march toward them.

"How does the officiant enter?"

Depending on custom, the formality of the wedding, and personal preference, the officiant either awaits the processional at the front of the church or marches at the head of the processional.

"When and how do the groomsmen and bridesmaids enter?"

In Protestant, Catholic, and nondenominational services, the wedding party usually enters first in the processional, coming from the back of the church. An alternative is for them to enter with the groom and his honor attendant at the front of the church. In some Jewish processionals the groomsmen follow the groom's grandparents up the aisle.

"Are the groomsmen supposed to enter alone or accompanied by bridesmaids?"

Both traditions are popular. In very formal weddings they tend to enter in separate groups — bridesmaids, groomsmen. Otherwise, it's more a matter of personal preference and the particular religious tradition of your faith.

"What if we have a different number of groomsmen than bridemaids?"

If you have an extra groomsman or bridesmaid, he or she would walk in alone, ahead of the rest.

"In what order should we place the attendants?"

If they are entering in separate groups, they are usually paired by height, the shortest in front, tallest in back. If you have an uneven number, the shortest would walk in alone, ahead of the other pairs.

"Must the bridesmaids enter in pairs?"

If you have more than four, they usually enter in pairs. Otherwise they enter alone, one following the next.

"How does the junior bridesmaid enter?"

She would precede the honor attendant, which would place her after the bridesmaids.

"What if there are two junior bridesmaids? Should they enter together?"

They may enter individually or together.

"Where does the honor attendant walk?"

The honor attendant walks in front of the flower girl and ring bearer. The flower girl and the ring bearer walk directly in front of the bride.

"What if there are two honor attendants? May they walk up the aisle together?"

Yes. Or you can have them in a single file, with the elder first.

"Does the ring bearer walk before or after the flower girl?"

He may either walk next to the flower girl or walk alone in front of the flower girl.

"May both of my parents be in the processional?"

Yes. It's a nice alternative.

"May the groom's parents be in the processional?"

It's up to the couple and the officiant. If the couple wishes for their parents to be in the processional, there's no reason why they shouldn't be. In traditional Jewish processionals they always participate.

"May I have both my father and stepfather escort me in the processional?"

It's the bride's father's privilege to "give" his daughter away. If you're considering this alternative, it's important to discuss it with him. Ideally he will be open to your wishes. If he responds negatively, it can make things awkward for everyone involved.

"May I ask my grandfather or brother to give me away?"

If your father is deceased or if for some reason he is unable to attend the ceremony, you may select any relative for the honor. Whom are you closest to? Who would appreciate the honor the most? That would be the one to choose.

"If there are two center aisles, which do we use?"

You may either close one of them off or use one (the left) for the processional and the other (right) for the recessional.

"May the groom and I walk up the aisle together?"

If the wedding is very informal or if you are significantly older, many couples follow this custom.

"Must we have a processional?"

In very small ceremonies, the couple usually just stands before the officiant. The honor attendants and guests stand around them. In larger weddings, they are customary. Formal weddings are very traditional. If yours will be informal, it is your decision.

"What is the order for the recessional?"

After the ceremony, in most cases, the recessional leaves in reverse order of the processional, with the bride and groom walking together at the end. After they leave the ushers traditionally "bow out" each row of guests, beginning at the front by bowing to let them know it is their time to file out.

Receiving Line

"What is the point of a receiving line?"

It's the most efficient way to greet your guests and make them feel welcome. Usually one forms after the ceremony, sometimes at the beginning of the reception. You decide. Some couples feel that it's too formal, and prefer to circulate among the guests. Unless the gathering is small and informal, they seldom succeed. The distractions of the day inevitably result in missing a chance to speak with some of the guests. With a receiving line, you know you will have seen all of your guests at least once.

"How do we line up after the ceremony?"

The traditional line up is:

- ◆ Hostess (usually bride's mother)
- ◆ Groom's mother
- ◆ Bride
- ◆ Groom
- ◆ Maid of honor
- ◆ Best man
- ◆ Bridesmaids and groomsmen are optional. It's your decision.

"Do our fathers stand in the receiving line?"

Fathers of the bride and groom rarely stand in the receiving line. If they do, the order would be:

- Bride's mother
- Groom's father
- Groom's mother
- Bride's father
- Bride
- Groom
- Maid of honor
- Best man
- Bridesmaids and groomsmen are optional. It's your decision.

"Is it necessary for the attendants to stand in the receiving line?"

The bride and groom make that decision. Although it's not a rule of etiquette, many times they are also family members and it's a chance for them to greet everyone, too.

"Do children in the wedding party stand in receiving lines?"

No.

"Our moms are not sure what they are supposed to do in the receiving line. Any suggestions?"

As official hostess for the day, your mom is introducing your family and loved ones to her counterpart in your new husband's family. The groom's mom is politely introducing his family and loved ones to the hostess, your mom.

"What do I say to people in the receiving line?"

Most of the time it will be a simple "thank you." The line will move quickly, and guests will be congratulating and complimenting. Occasionally you will be introduced to someone by your new husband and you would simply say, "how nice to meet you."

"What if I don't know the person, and they aren't being introduced?"

Smile nicely and ask them their name.

"What is the proper way to introduce people?"

There is a large, detailed section on how to handle introductions in chapter 8, "Manners 101."

"Does someone say 'congratulations' or 'best wishes' to the bride?"

In traditional weddingspeak, one offers "best wishes" to the bride before the ceremony. After the ceremony she is congratulated. The groom is always congratulated because he won the heart of a wonderful woman!

6

Military
Wedding

"What is a military wedding?"

Local protocol varies, so check with your commanding officer before making your plans.

In general it is for officers who marry in dress uniform. Those retired or in the reserve may still choose to have a military wedding. The ceremony site is traditionally a military church or chapel, with a chaplain officiating. (Traditionally the chaplain isn't paid for this service.) An American flag and the standards of your military unit(s) are displayed during the ceremony.

"What sort of military wedding may an enlisted person have?"

An enlisted person may marry in uniform, but the rest of the celebration would follow civilian traditions. Traditionally if the bride is the enlisted person, she still wears a bridal gown.

Uniforms and Proper Attire

"Can other members of the wedding party wear their military uniforms if the bride and groom are in civilian clothes?"

That would be up to the bride and groom.

"Can a female officer marry in uniform?"

Yes, or she can select a traditional bridal gown.

"Is it proper for the best man to wear his formal military uniform when the rest of the groomsmen will be wearing tuxedos?"

If the groom will be in uniform, or the couple specifically request that he wear it, that's acceptable. Some might feel it would detract attention from the groom if the best man was the only man in the wedding party in uniform.

"What uniform is proper for a formal wedding?"

It depends on the formality, and whether the officer is commissioned. An officer's evening dress uniform is considered the equivalent of "white tie and tails" in civilian attire. Their dinner dress uniform would be worn if civilians are wearing "black tie" attire.

"Can women wear corsages or men wear boutonnieres on their uniforms?"

No, flowers or other such additions are never worn on a military uniform.

"If a guest is a member of the military, are they required to wear their uniforms to a military wedding?"

It's their choice, unless it's required by local protocol, or specifically requested by the bride and groom.

Special Customs

"How is seating different?"

Rank is carefully observed when seating guests. Generals would be in the front, followed by sergeants, privates behind the sergeants, and recruits in the back.

"Is the bride still on the left side?"

Yes, unless the groom is a male officer wearing a sword or saber. These are worn on the left side. In that case, the bride and her attendants stand on the right.

The Arch of Sabers or Swords

"What is the 'arch of swords' or 'arch of sabers'?"

A tradition for officers who choose a military wedding style. After the recessional, guests are invited outside before the bride and groom leave the ceremony location so they may view the proceedings. An arch is formed by attendants and invited guests in formal dress uniforms and white gloves. Usually there are six or eight sword/saber bearers. On command they raise their blades (facing up and away from the couple) and form an arch with tips nearly touching.

"How is the newly married couple announced before they walk through the arch of sabers?"

The senior usher announces: "Ladies and Gentlemen, it is my honor to present to you . . . "

If only the groom is in the military, the groom's rank is announced. For example: "Captain and Mrs. Johnson." If the bride is also in the military, both ranks are announced. For example: "Major and Captain Johnson."

"What is the protocol for walking through the arch of sabers?"

After the couple is announced by the senior usher, they proceed through the arch. Traditionally the last two bearers lower their blades to keep the couple in the arch. If the bride is not also in the military, the left sword/saber bearer gives the bride a swat on the rear end with the saber and says, "Welcome to the [army or navy or whichever branch of service her husband is in]." After the bride and groom pass through, the team is commanded to dissolve its formation.

"What if some of my ushers are not in the military?"

These ushers would stand at attention in the line.

"Do we cut the cake differently?"

Yes. The groom cuts the cake with his sword or saber.

7

The Reception

"What do we do after the ceremony if we are not having a reception?"

After the recessional, form a receiving line to greet your guests and thank them for coming.

"What occurs at the reception?"

The actual activities vary to some degree, but the point is always the same. It's a celebratory gathering to receive the new couple into the community. Usually some food, drink, and fellowship are involved. Larger receptions might include a full meal, music, and dancing. Traditionally the couple cuts the cake together. Then the bride tosses her bouquet of flowers into a gathering of unmarried females and the groom tosses the bride's garter to nonmarried males.

Choosing Your Reception Style

The time of day, type of entertainment, and refreshments define the style of reception. It should also be suitable to the formality or informality of the wedding ceremony.

Breakfast

A breakfast gathering after an early morning ceremony might include wedding cake and champagne for dessert. It is, after all, a very special occasion!

Luncheon

The celebration begins between 12 and 2 P.M. Guests enjoy salads, sandwiches, and finger foods. Beverages might include soda pop, tea, coffee, punch, and alcoholic drinks. The couple cuts the cake at the end of the meal. Guests enjoy it as dessert and then depart.

Cake and Punch

Many couples opt for this if they are having a small gathering between 2 and 5 P.M. Guests are served wedding cake and simple beverages such as punch, tea, or coffee. Sometimes this is called a tea reception.

Cocktail

Traditionally they begin around 5 P.M., never later than 6 P.M. It is often used as a cost-effective alternative to an expensive dinner reception. Guests are served hors d'oeuvres and beverages. Many couples select a few alcoholic and nonalcoholic drinks offered through the bar.

If you are planning this style, make sure that your guests understand that a full meal will not be served. Cutting the cake and serving it as dessert is considered the highlight of this type of reception.

Dinner

Food costs in a dinner reception almost always represent the largest portion of the wedding expense. A buffet dinner, where guests serve themselves and carry their plates to their seats, is less expensive. A sit-down dinner, where food is brought to the table, is the expected tradition when you have a formal wedding. Dinner receptions begin between 6 and 8 P.M. Sometimes a cocktail hour precedes the dinner. The cake is cut and served after dinner. There is usually music and dancing as part of the celebration.

Belated Reception

Sometimes the couple has eloped and other times a family crisis forced the newlyweds to delay their celebration. A belated reception is one that takes place after the date of the wedding ceremony. The bride and groom wear their wedding attire, and the customary traditions (toasts, cake, music, meal, etc.) can all be enjoyed. The premise is as if the couple had been married on that day.

Second Reception

If the marriage celebration took place far from the family and friends of either the bride or groom, a second reception might be held so that those loved ones can also celebrate the marriage. Its level of formality does not have to duplicate that of the original reception. However there's no reason that it shouldn't.

Dinner Seating Arrangements

"Why does the wedding party sit at an elevated head table facing everyone?"

It makes it easier for guests to see them, and it makes it seem like they are at everyone else's table.

"How do I arrange the wedding party at the head table?"

The bride and the groom are at the center with the honor attendants flanking them. Bridesmaids, groomsmen, and ushers would also be seated there. They are seated in a male/female pattern.

"What is a 'sweetheart table'?"

If the couple prefers not to have the entire wedding party seated at one table, they can opt for this solution. The bride and groom sit together facing their guests. Sometimes the table is slightly elevated to make it easier for guests to see the couple. The wedding party and close family sit at other tables nearby.

"Do children in the wedding party sit at the head table?"

Children who are in the wedding party are seldom seated at the head table, unless they are older and well behaved.

"Where are our parents seated?"

If there is room, parents of the bride and groom may be seated at the head table. If not, they are seated at an honor table.

"Neither set of parents wants to sit at the head table. Where are our parents seated?"

Separate honor tables might include parents, grandparents, officiant, siblings, children, and others very close to the couple.

"How do we indicate who sits where?"

Fewer weddings these days have place cards for guest dinner

seating, but they're still practical for honor seating. Use place cards in those locations to avoid confusion and embarrassment.

> **"My parents are divorced. May I have two honor tables**
> **so they won't have to sit together?"**

There's nothing wrong with having more than one honor table. If you both have large families, it will be a necessity.

> **"I want to have place cards at each dinner setting. How**
> **do I determine the seating arrangements?"**

Alternate men and women in every other chair. Keep those who don't get along separate. Try not to put anyone at a table made up entirely of strangers. Avoid seating elderly people too close to the musicians. Combine groupings so that everyone has an opportunity to meet someone new. Be conscious that those who have traveled long distances will be looking forward to visiting their friends and relatives.

> **"I'm picturing mass confusion as three hundred guests**
> **try to find their place cards. What can I do to help guests**
> **find their proper seats?"**

Number the tables and have the caterer put place cards at each setting. Place a large seating chart near the guest book that lists everyone's names alphabetically, followed by their table numbers.

> **"Where should I seat spouses of members of the wedding**
> **party?"**

They are usually seated dispersed among the rest of the guests.

"If our meal is served buffet-style, may I still have the wedding party served seated?"

It would be very unusual to see the bride and groom standing in line with their plates. They and the wedding party are traditionally served seated. Your guests will expect it to be that way.

Toasts

"Who offers the first toast at the engagement party?"

The bride's father. He traditionally wishes the couple a lifetime of happiness together.

"Who offers the first toast at the rehearsal dinner?"

The groom's father begins, followed by the best man. Usually everyone in the wedding party offers a toast to the happy couple.

"Who offers the first toast at the reception?"

The best man toasts the newlyweds. Other toasts may follow then, or later during the festivities. Usually the groom then toasts his bride, she offers him a toast in return. Together they toast their parents and guests. Other attendants, parents, friends, or relatives might also choose to toast the newly married pair.

"When does the toasting begin?"

Prewedding parties: Prior to the meal or other festivities.
Reception: At smaller gatherings or cocktail receptions, the

toasting begins after the receiving line breaks up. At a dinner reception, it follows the blessing and precedes the meal.

"What do you say?"

A toast is best kept short, simple, and sincere. It should sound straight from the heart. The person(s) making the toast should speak clearly and loud enough so all can hear. The toaster asks the others to rise and join him or her in a toast. They refer to the person being toasted and offer a short complimentary wish towards him or her. When the toast is finished, the toaster raises his or her glass so people know the toast is finished.

"How do you toast?"

When the verbal tribute is finished, neighbors clink their glasses and sip.

"What do I do when I am being toasted?"

You acknowledge the honor by nodding and smiling at the person offering the toast to you. You do not stand (unless everyone is standing), sip, or raise your glass.

"Must we use alcoholic beverages to toast?"

No, any beverage is fine. There should always be a nonalcoholic alternative available for guests who do not drink.

"My fiancé's mother died last year, and he wants to include a toast to her at the reception. Is that OK?"

It's wonderful that your fiancé wants to honor his mother. However, a wedding is a celebration among the living—and not the time or place to toast the deceased.

Alcoholic Beverages

Whether to serve alcohol, what kind, and for how long can represent a mine field of problems for many couples. Here are a few important rules to follow to keep your lives simple.

1. You don't have to serve alcohol.
2. If you do, limit the drink options.
3. Remember to include nonalcoholic cocktail choices too.
4. Don't have a cash bar.

"Why shouldn't I have a cash bar for the alcoholic beverages?"

You invited guests to celebrate with you. As part of the invitation, you offered refreshments—whether it's cake and punch or a three-course meal. These traditions have continued since ancient times. It's only recently that some couples have had the audacity to insult their guests by asking them to pay for some of the refreshments of the party. If you can't afford it, don't offer it.

"My uncle has a drinking problem. How should we handle that?"

It's hard to leave a close relative out of such a celebration. Such a decision will inevitably result in hurt feelings and possible family feuds. Realistically, just talking to someone will not guarantee good behavior. Although if you or your mother feel comfortable trying, it may help. If you do, avoid being confrontational. Just state your fears and the reasons behind them. Ask him to make a special effort to avoid a scene. If you have someone who has a positive outlook, knows your uncle, and could have some influence on him, you might ask the person to keep an eye on your uncle for the evening.

Blessing or Grace

If you have a religious ceremony, it's customary to have a prayer before your meal. However if religious beliefs are somehow an issue among your families, you have the option of asking for a moment of silent reflection and thanksgiving before the meal begins. If it's a civil ceremony and you and your husband are not religious, any prayers would be entirely at your discretion.

"Who says grace?"

If your officiant will be present, it's customary to ask him or her to offer a prayer. Otherwise the best man, your honor attendant, friend, or anyone you choose may do it. However, prepare whomever you choose ahead of time. Don't spring it on him or her five minutes before the meal will begin.

"How do we say grace?"

The prayer is said before the meal is begun. The person saying the prayer advises the gathering to stand or sit, hold hands or fold hands, and usually to bow their heads. They then offer words of gratitude for the meal and the celebratory gathering.

Music and Dancing

"*Are we required to have music?*"

Musical accompaniment adds to the festivities no matter what your wedding style. The more formal and elaborate the wedding is, the more music you would have. Music is expected but not required.

"*How do we decide what kind of music to have?*"

It depends on budget, preference, and the style of reception. For example:

* Small, informal: CD in the background
* Large, formal: A pianist, violinist, or flutist would play softly during the meal. A live band with a DJ backup would perform during the dancing.

Most weddings fall somewhere between the two.

"*Is there a special order to the dancing?*"

Typically:

1. Dancing begins with the bride and groom dancing slowly to a meaningful romantic song.
2. After a few minutes it's customary for the bride's father to cut in, and the groom dances with the bride's mother.
3. Then the groom's father dances with the bride and the groom with his mother.

4. The honor attendants and then all the wedding party join in.

5. Then the guests come out on the floor.

"We don't know how to slow dance. What should we do?"

That first dance together is a very strong tradition. It will be hard to ignore or disregard the custom. You may find yourselves being prodded and teased if you try to leave it out. Practice waltzing now. If you aren't able to practice, the time-honored alternative is to just hold each other and sway back and forth a little bit.

"How do we select music that people of all ages can enjoy?"

It's good that you are concerned about entertaining all of your guests. Talk to your musicians or DJ. They'll be experienced in helping you to select the songs that will receive the best responses on the dance floor. Another option is to ask people of different age groups the names of their favorite tunes. Each decade has plenty of melodies with a good beat that will inspire listeners to move their feet.

8

Manners 101

Ten Tips for Introductions

1. Always introduce people who may not know each other.
2. Introduce less important to more important.
3. Introduce younger to older.
4. Introduce a man to a woman.
5. You introduce by saying, "Guest A, I would like to introduce you to Guest B."
6. When being introduced, nod or smile and say hello.
7. When you are introduced, repeat the name back to help you remember it.
8. Do not address people who are significantly older or of higher rank (such as a governor or senator) by their first names.
9. Address professionals that are providing services by their last names, not their first. For example: Mrs. Peabody, the florist.
10. Always introduce someone by their full name.

The Proper Way to Introduce Someone

"How would my mother introduce my husband's parents?"

"May I present my son-in-law's parents, Mr. and Mrs. Gabriel?" or "I'd like you to meet John's parents, Mr. and Mrs. Gabriel."

Here are a few examples for some trickier situations.

Stepmother

"This is my stepmother, Isabelle Herrera."

Stepchild

"This is my stepson, Tyler Weaver."

Sister-in-Law

"This is Kelly, Jeff's wife."

Widowed Sister-in-Law

"I'd like you to meet Elizabeth Denton. She is my brother Dave's widow."

Former Sister-in-Law

"I would like you to meet Caroline Schumacker. She was Christopher's wife and is now married to Zachary Schumacker."

Former Mother-in-Law

"This is Mrs. Galloway, my first husband's mother." Or, "This is Mrs. Galloway. She's Cara's grandmother."

Brother's Live-in Girlfriend

"This is Janelle, she's the wonderful woman who lives with my brother Alexander."

Introducing a Man to a Woman

"Mrs. Heath, this is my husband, Jeffrey Landstrom."

Introducing Two Women (Younger to Older)

"Aunt Amelia, may I present my friend Makayla."

Introducing Two Men of the Same Age (Less Important to More Important)

"Governor Jones, I'd like you to meet James Francis."

Introducing an Important Family Member to a Friend

"Mr. Gustafson, may I present my sister, Dr. Melanie Stevens?"

All About Names

"Must I take my husband's name?"

No, not usually. In most cases it's a cultural tradition, not a legal one.

"What is the difference between Miss, Mrs., and Ms.?"

The first two have always been tied to marital status. "Miss Lane" is an unmarried woman. "Mrs. Lane" is a married woman. "Ms. Lane" is a social title, indicating that the person is female, but not connected to marital status.

"What do I call my husband's parents?"

This is a very personal choice; ideally your in-laws should indicate their preference. Mr. or Mrs. is cold and rather formal. Consider using a different form of mother or father than you use for own parents—mom, dad, mama, papa. Your in-laws might request that you use their first names. Another alternative is to use their last name initial, such as Mr. & Mrs. B.

"What do I call my new husband's other relatives, such as his aunts and uncles?"

You refer to them the same way that your spouse does: "Uncle Joe," "Aunt Jane." If you are formally introducing them, you would say something like, "Senator Brownstone, this is David's uncle, Maxwell Ollesini."

"My honor attendant is a widow. Is she a maid or matron of honor?"

She's a matron of honor. It doesn't matter if she still is married, just that she was married once.

"My first husband is deceased. What should my two children call their stepfather?"

It's best to let the children decide. Don't force a version of dad or daddy on them. If they don't want to use a variation of the title father, a nickname or his first name are also acceptable.

"What should my stepdaughter call me?"

If her mother is still living, try to help her to select a variation of mother that she doesn't use with her living parent. She could call you by your first name or a special nickname would be acceptable.

"How do I inform people that I have kept my maiden name?"

Enclose a card with your wedding invitations or announcements. It may say "Amanda Crossley will retain her maiden name for all legal and social purposes after the marriage."

"I don't like the way our names sound when they are hyphenated; however, I want to keep my name, too. What are alternatives to hyphenating our names?"

You might use your maiden name as your middle name. Or each of you can keep your own name.

"If we hyphenate, how do we decide which order to put the names in?"

Most couples choose the order that sounds the best.

"If we hyphenate our names, do we both use the hyphenated name?"

Yes. If you hyphenate, you should both use the hyphenated format.

"I want children. If I don't take his name, what name will our children have?"

If you keep your maiden name, your children can take either name—although traditionally they have the husband's name. If you hyphenate, children's names can be hyphenated, too. Or some parents choose to give the wife's maiden name to the children as a middle name. With so many alternative name choices and repeat marriages, many children travel through life with a different last name than their mothers.

> *"I was shopping with my maid of honor and encountered a distant aunt. I couldn't think of her name even though I had just mailed her an invitation. I'm embarrassed to admit that I hid behind a rack of clothes because I didn't know how to handle it. What should I do if I can't remember a person's name?"*

Here are a few suggestions:

- "Auntie, have you met Jane Doe?" Hopefully, your aunt would offer her name when she extends her hand to Jane.
- "I'm sorry auntie, my mind is full of wedding plans and I can't think of my own name today or yours. This is my maid of honor, Jane Doe." Hopefully, your aunt would offer her name when she extends her hand to Jane.

Meal Manners

Do you know how to properly use your dinner utensils? Are you clear on how to eat chicken at a wedding? Casual dining and rare family meals have resulted in a lack of experience with proper table manners. Once you're clear on the more formal "rules," it will be easier to adapt to any situation. A formal dinner is specifically seven courses, served in the following order: soup, fish, sorbet, meat or poultry, salad, dessert, coffee/tea. The place setting can be intimidating in both personal and business situations. Here are some basics:

Three General Rules

1. Your dinner plate is the center of the setting.
2. Liquids on the right, solids on the left.
3. Use silverware from the outside to inside.

Basic table manners rely on behavior that will not cause discomfort to fellow diners. Most people learn the following as young children, yet there are still too many who need this lesson:

Five Commandments for the Table

1. Do not show fellow diners the food in your mouth. Avoid talking or drinking while you are chewing.
2. Do not wave silverware around when you speak.
3. Do not make noises when you eat or drink (slurping, gulping, etc.).
4. Do not groom yourself by picking your teeth, combing your hair, or applying makeup.
5. Do not return food to the serving dish after you have touched it with your personal utensils or placed it on your plate.

Silverware Savvy

At the table setting:

- Knives and spoons are set on the right side of the plate.
- Napkin and forks are placed to the left of the plate; salad fork is on the outermost left.

◆ Dessert utensils are set above the dinner plate or
brought out with dessert.

Once you have used a utensil, do not put it back on the table.
Place it on the plate or saucer.

Any unused silverware is left on the table.

Napkin Signals

The meal begins when the host or hostess unfolds their napkin. It's your signal to do the same. Smaller napkins are completely
unfolded, large dinner napkins are folded lengthwise. It remains in
your lap throughout the meal.

If you need to leave the table during the meal, place the napkin
on your chair. The meal ends when the host/hostess places his/her
napkin on the table. When you have finished eating, place yours
neatly on the table next to your dinner plate.

The Proper Way to Eat Specific Foods

Soup

Tilt the spoon away from you when you fill it. Sip from the side
of the spoon. Don't make noise.

Bread

Break the bread into smaller portions with your fingers. Butter
each portion, then eat it before you butter the next.

Finger Foods

Celery, pickles, radishes, pitted olives, and carrot sticks.

Place them on the side of your dinner plate. You can eat them with your fingers, but eat them in small bites. When eating an olive, gently move the pit from your mouth to your hand and place the pit on the edge of your plate.

Salad

If the salad is the main entrée, or served as a side dish on your main dinner plate, you use your dinner fork. Otherwise use your salad fork. If vegetables in the salad are too large to place on a fork, it's fine to cut them up.

Meat

Always cut and eat one small piece at a time. Unless you're at a picnic or informal gathering, chicken, turkey legs, spareribs, and other such items are eaten with a knife and fork.

Caviar

Spread it on a bite size piece of toast. Add onions or capers as preferred.

Lobster and Crabs

Use a nutcracker to crack the shell, pull the meat out with a seafood fork. If the piece is large, cut it before eating.

9

Giving and Receiving Gifts

Gifts for You

"Will we receive a gift in response to every invitation?"

Gift giving is meant to be an open expression of joy. It has become so customary at weddings that it is "expected." You invite guests to share your celebration. You are expected to show good manners by being surprised by the giver's generosity. Sadly there are couples that pad their guest lists by sending invitations to everyone they have ever met. The idea is that those who know proper etiquette will feel an obligation to send something. This blatant appeal for gifts is always recognized by the receiver. It is considered "improper" etiquette to send such an invitation. If they don't know you well, they will not buy you a present.

"If we elope will we still receive gifts?"

No one has an obligation to send a gift in this case. Some people will give you a gift anyway if they are especially close. Traditionally couples who elope do not receive wedding gifts.

"I was married before. Will I still receive wedding gifts?"

No one is obligated to provide a gift at a second wedding. Your immediate family and very close friends will probably present you with gifts. Many guests will still give a gift, most likely on a smaller scale than the one offered at your first wedding.

"Are monetary gifts considered rude?"

No. In some communities and ethnic cultures it's a tradition to give money as a gift.

"Is there anything wrong with specifying that we prefer monetary gifts?"

Yes. Any hint of "asking" for a gift is considered rude. The popularity of wedding gift registries has confused the issue. A basic rule is that you, your future spouse, your parents, or anyone close to you do not "suggest" anything about a gift UNLESS someone specifically asks. Then preferences can be mentioned. In most regions it's still considered poor manners to request financial gifts.

"We hope to receive a certain amount of money from each guest to cover our wedding expenses. Would it be wrong to mention a minimum cash amount for our gifts?"

It would be very wrong. The amount a guest spends on a gift is based on the closeness and affection they have for the bride and/or groom and what they can afford. The cost of the wedding and the couple's ability to pay for it have nothing to do with the value of gifts they will receive. In polite society it is assumed that you will not put on a celebration that you cannot afford.

"Is it OK to return a gift I don't like? Should I ask the gift giver for a receipt?"

First the gift giver must indicate that it would be fine with them if you wish to return the item. In such cases they will offer the receipt. You should never ask. And if they don't offer, you should not return the gift. Duplicate gifts however can be exchanged at the store they came from. If you don't know the store you should not ask. The giver should offer a receipt.

Displaying Wedding Gifts

"May we display gifts at the reception?"

Traditionally gifts are displayed at the bride's parents' home before the wedding. This custom is seldom practiced anymore. It is rare, primarily for security reasons, to display the gifts at the reception site. However if you do display gifts, you should have someone watching the table. Many couples hire a security guard in such circumstances.

"How are gifts displayed?"

Display the gifts on tables covered with simple cloths. Place each in an attractive position, with items of similar quality together — an item's inexpensiveness will be glaring if it's among expensive items. Some people separate the gifts by type—china, glassware, or silverware—or by color, pattern, shapes, or textures. Duplicates should be scattered as far apart as possible.

"How do we note monetary gifts if we display our presents?"

You may use a list or individual cards that say: "Check from Mr. and Mrs. Del Giorno" or "Monetary gift from George Whitley."

"How should I handle a gift that arrives broken?"

If a gift arrives broken, check the return address. If it came directly from the store, notify the store. If the guest mailed an insured package, notify the gift giver so he or she may place a claim.

"I've heard that guests can send a gift up to a year after the wedding date. Is that proper?"

Yes, according to tradition the guest has 12 months. The basis is that they may be traveling, distracted by personal matters, or in difficult financial circumstances at the time of your wedding.

"A mutual friend offered to take the wedding photographs as his gift to us. We know he can't afford much, but we prefer to hire a professional photographer. What should we do?"

Explain that you'll look forward to his gift of providing a personal perspective of the day but that you have also hired a professional photographer to cover the wedding. After all, you want this good friend to be able to join in the celebration, too.

Gift Registry

"We need to register for our wedding gifts. What type of gifts should I register for?"

Generally you register for items that will help you furnish your new home. Most couples focus on kitchen, dining room, and decorative items they will enjoy. This might include cookware, monogrammed glassware, framed oil paintings, or a set of lamps. Older, more settled couples are often given a themed shower that reflects their interests. For example: ardent campers would receive helpful outdoor gear.

"My fiancé is divorced, but I have never been married. Should we still register for gifts?"

Yes. Since household items are still considered the domain of the bride, this is your opportunity to select your preferences for your new home.

"I was married before, but my fiancé was not. Should we still register for gifts?"

Traditionally it's assumed that the female received most of the household items in any divorce. In second marriages, most couples register for items based on a theme.

"We don't need basic household items. What should we suggest when people ask about possible gifts?"

Ask for things you would not usually buy for yourselves and might enjoy. Some ideas include a selection of gourmet foods such as imported cheeses, coffee, and tea; a fine bottle of wine or champagne; a tree or shrub for your garden; or something that adds to a hobby or collection you enjoy.

"Should my registry information be included with the invitations?"

A gift is supposed to be offered freely. Therefore you aren't supposed to "suggest" what gift to buy. Retailers created this trend by encouraging couples to register to "help" guests with their choices. Many guests rely on the registry to ensure they purchase an item the couple really wants or needs. However, good manners require that you (or anyone) only offer a list of your registries when a person specifically asks for it.

Wedding Showers

The tradition began as a way to help young couples accumulate items to set up housekeeping. Though many of today's couples already have the basics, this tradition continues. Often the parties are for a certain theme, such as entertainment or gourmet cooking. It's still considered extremely rude to ask for gifts of money.

"Who will give me a wedding shower?"

Traditionally the maid of honor, with assistance from the other female attendants throw at least one. Members of the groom's family, coworkers, and other friends might also sponsor additional showers.

"What if all of my close friends are family members? Does this mean that I may not have a shower?"

No, this is an exceptional situation. The idea behind the tradition is that the bride's family shouldn't look as though they are soliciting gifts. If her friends give the bride a shower, it is supposed to seem less calculating.

"I've been told that the maid of honor sponsors the wedding shower. I've also been told that immediate family members do not sponsor showers. What if my sister is my maid of honor?"

She is sponsoring the shower as your maid of honor, not as your sister.

"What's the difference between a wedding shower and a bridal shower?"

In many cases they are the same, just called by a different name in certain regions. In some areas, a woman receives more personal (and sometimes naughty) gifts at her bridal shower. At the wedding shower the gifts are for both the bride and groom.

"When is the shower held?"

Showers are usually held one to two months before the wedding date. The last few weeks before the wedding are much too hectic for parties.

"My friends have said that they are giving me a shower, but no one has asked me for a guest list. Should I offer one?"

Unless it's a surprise party, the bride or her mother usually provides a list of guests, upon request. You might discreetly check with your mom first. If she hasn't been asked for a list and the wedding is less than two months away, it wouldn't be improper for her to contact your friends and ask about any shower plans.

"I'm having several bridal showers. May I ask the same people to more than one?"

Only your maid of honor, attendants, and immediate family (mother, grandmothers, siblings) should be invited to every shower.

"I've been married before, may I still have a shower?"

How long has it been since your first wedding? If it has been at least three years, a simple, low-key shower would not be considered improper. Rather than suggesting the more traditional shower gifts, a themed shower for a particular interest of yours would be more appropriate.

"Should my fiancé attend the shower?"

Traditionally only the bride attends the shower. However many men attend their wedding showers for two reasons: the gifts are now given to the bride *and* groom, and in many instances this will be the first time many family members will meet him. However if he absolutely refuses to attend, no one should be offended.

"What is a 'Jack and Jill shower'?"

The groom isn't the only male present and most female attendees bring dates. Gifts are given to the couple. The customary shower format of party games and favors is seldom used. After the gifts are opened, it tends to carry on like any other party.

"I feel more comfortable throwing a shower for myself. Won't my friends be happy that I'm making their lives easier?"

It's a huge breach of etiquette to throw your own shower, because the point of the party is to give presents to the bride.

Gifts From You

"My engagement ring is a gift from my fiancé. Do I give him a gift in return?"

It's not a widespread tradition, but some women choose to give their fiancé a gift at the same time. The gift is usually a simple item of jewelry, such as cuff links, a watch, or a key chain.

"Do we give gifts to our wedding party?"

Yes. Shortly before the wedding each attendant should receive a gift. Traditionally these are given at the rehearsal dinner. Gifts are usually some permanent, personal memento of the occasion. Typically, a monogrammed piece of jewelry, a picture frame, or perhaps a special item handmade by you. Gifts to the honor attendants are slightly nicer than gifts that other attendants receive.

"Are we required to give each guest a gift in the form of 'favors,' such as candies or scrolls with our names and wedding date inscribed?"

No, favors are just a friendly way to offer each person who joined your celebration a memento of the occasion.

Tips and Gratuities for the Wedding

"Why should I tip?"

In many service industries, especially among food and beverage providers, employees are paid a very small wage. They are expected to make the bulk of their income from tips. The tips are an additional incentive for providing efficient, gracious service.

"Who distributes the gratuities?"

Either the best man (or honor attendant for the groom), reception host, or the wedding consultant.

"Do I always have to leave a tip?"

No. If the gratuity has already been added to your bill, or if the service was bad, tipping is not necessary.

"What is the percentage rule of thumb?"

The fancier the location and occasion, the bigger the compensation. Generally, 15 to 20 percent.

"What is an easy way to compute tips?"

- A 15 percent tip equals 10 percent plus half.
- A 20 percent tip equals 10 percent times two.

"How do I indicate to guests that all tips have been prepaid?"

Display signs stating, "The host has prepaid all gratuities," in appropriate locations.

"Who is tipped and how much?"

If gratuities are not included in the contract:

- Bartender, limo driver, waitpersons: 15–20 percent of the bill
- Cloakroom attendant: $1.00 per item
- Musicians: host tips each musician $20.00, guests tip $2.00 per special request
- Valet parking: $2.00 per car

10

Saying Thank You

Gift Acknowledgment Cards

"May I send a preprinted card acknowledging that a gift has been received?"

Acknowledgment cards do not replace thank-you notes. Their purpose is to buy time and notify the sender that you have received their gift. You are still expected to send a personal thank-you note as soon as possible after the honeymoon.

"How are acknowledgment cards worded?"

Here is a suggestion:

> Mr. and Mrs. Jackson Zaharias
> gratefully acknowledge the receipt of your wedding gift
> and offer their sincere thanks.

Thank-You Cards

"I am too busy to write thank-you notes."

Your guests are busy people too. They shared a portion of their income in providing a gift for you. In many cases they took time to purchase and wrap it too. They also used their precious time and money to attend the wedding and reception. That might include costs for clothing, travel, and a babysitter. All to help make your day special and to join in your celebration.

Taking a little of your own time to write a personal note in return is not just good manners, it's the least you could do in return.

"When am I obligated to send a thank-you note?"

For any party where you are a guest of honor, send a note to everyone who gave or helped with the party. You must also send a note for every shower and wedding gift, even if you have thanked the gift giver in person.

"May I send a thank-you note for a wedding gift before the wedding?"

Yes. Ideally you'll send out your notes as soon as each gift is received. That way you won't have a large pile to write after the honeymoon.

"If I send a note before the wedding, do I sign my maiden name or married name?"

Sign all notes before the wedding with your maiden name, and after the wedding with your married name.

"Should we sign both of our names to the thank-you note?"

Yes. Most couples sign their notes with both names.

Deadline for Mailing

"How long do I have after the wedding to send out the thank-you notes?"

Guests begin to expect them after the honeymoon. Ideally they will be mailed within one month of your wedding date. No matter what the circumstances, they should still be completed and mailed within three months after the wedding.

"We have a wedding Web site. It would be easier on our budget to simply post a big thank you to all of our guests after the wedding. Isn't that more practical?"

There's nothing wrong with that, but the posting would not replace individual thank-you notes. Good manners require hand-written notes. There aren't any shortcuts.

Help with the Wording

"What information should be included in the thank-you note?"

Refer to the gift and how it will be used. Say something to show that you appreciate the time and money used to acquire it.

"When thanking a husband and wife simultaneously, whom do I address the note to?"

Traditionally the wife sends a gift to the bride. The bride writes a note thanking the wife. The husband is mentioned in the text of the note. Today most gifts are sent to the bride and groom and signed by the husband and wife. In those cases you can address the note to the husband and wife.

"How is a traditional note worded?"

Here is an example:

Dear Sarah and Kevin,

Justin and I appreciate the wonderful cookware set you gave us on our wedding day.

The lovely blue enamel complements our kitchen perfectly.

We would love to have you both over for dinner soon, and you can see how well they work.

Once again, thank you for your generosity.

Sincerely,
Jennifer Tealson

"How do I thank someone for a bizarre gift?"

Such an item would be distinctive, charming, unique, or stunning—you might refer to "the distinctive blue clay pot" or "the stunning white ceramic figure." Tell the gift giver it will undoubtedly be in a special place in your new home.

"Do I write individual thank-you notes for group gifts?"

It depends on how the gift was presented. For a large group

gift from coworkers, a handwritten note to all on the office bulletin board and an individual "thank you" when you see the person will be sufficient. If each person in the group wrapped a portion (a place setting, for example) and signed that portion, then each should receive a thank-you note.

"Can I thank them for their shower and wedding gift in the same note?"

They should have received the thank-you for the shower gift before the wedding. They took the time to proffer two gifts. You should take the time to write two notes.

"When we receive a monetary gift, are we supposed to mention the amount in the note?"

Yes. It's also nice to add a description of how the money will be used.

"Is there anything wrong with computer-generated thank-you notes? Why?"

Yes, because you're supposed to take some time to write a personal note by hand.

"May I e-mail my thank-you notes?"

You're following tradition by having a wedding celebration. Part of the custom is to write a personal note of thanks.

"Do I send a thank-you to a guest who attended the wedding but did not give a gift?"

Yes. They still took the time to be a part of your celebration.

You should indicate gratitude for their presence. As mentioned previously, the guest has twelve months to send a gift. They may be planning to send something later. If they do, you send a thank-you for the item.

11

Controversial Subjects

Handling Difficult Situations

"We moved our wedding date forward two months. Too many people assume it means that I'm pregnant. How do I deal with this?"

Rude and frustrating rumors are impossible to control. Some people will always look for something to gossip about. They will look foolish when no baby is born on the predicted date.

"I will be visibly pregnant at our wedding. Should I tell people beforehand?"

Do you want to hear whispers of surprise following you up the aisle? Let the word out ahead of time.

"We're not even married and people are asking when we're having children. What do I tell them?"

It's amazing how many people feel perfectly comfortable inquiring about changes in your marital status and reproductive plans. Neither subject is anyone else's business, unless you decide to make it so. "We prefer not to discuss it right now" is the best answer to those inquiries.

"My fiancé is black; I am white. I'm afraid that some of my family members will be rude at the wedding to him or his family. What can I do?"

You can hope that your family is well mannered enough not to spoil your happiness. If you don't think they are capable of behaving decently, ask a levelheaded mutual friend or relative to talk to them about your concerns. Every family of every race, color, and creed has an occasional ill-mannered lout. Hopefully your fiancé's family will understand this if the worst happens.

"I am black; my fiancé is white. His family is very patronizing towards me. What can I do?"

Bigotry is based on ignorance. As time passes and you become an individual in their eyes, they should stop seeing race and start appreciating your individual qualities. The best response in the mean time is to ignore it, as you would any rude or boorish behavior.

"I'm marrying a significantly older man. His children are very uncomfortable around me. What can I do?"

You are stepping into a nontraditional role in his children's lives. You are not their mother, friend, or sibling. You are going to be their dad's wife. It must make them feel a little odd for their dad's wife to be of their generation. Give them time. As they get to know you as a person who loves and cares for their father, they will accept the person, not the age.

"My sister is a lesbian and wants to 'come out' at our wedding. I feel like it will ruin my wedding day because all of the focus will be on her situation. Am I right to object?"

Yes, you are right. Your sister may be thinking it would be a handy time, with all the family gathered all in one place. However the day that you are pledging to join your life with someone else's should not be disrupted by your sister's announcement of her sexual orientation. I would encourage her very strongly to break the ice beforehand rather than at your wedding. She can begin by informing immediate family members and let the grapevine do the rest.

12

When Bad Things Happen

Wedding Fears

"I've been having nightmares about being stood up at the altar. My fiancé assures me he has no plans to abandon me. I'm so terrified that it will happen I can barely sleep. Any suggestions?"

Everyone has such terrors. Too many movies have shown a bride or groom left standing at the altar before the ceremony. In reality it doesn't happen that often. If for some reason it does, he will look like a dim-witted, spineless creep. To allow the planning to continue and then, in the most cowardly way imaginable, bail out at the last minute is not only vile, it's immoral. If he's truly that deceitful, then he doesn't deserve you. It would be better for you to endure an hour of embarrassment and lose some deposits than to be legally bound in marriage to such a person.

"I have this horror that somehow my wedding gown will be destroyed before I make it to the altar. I envision spilling coffee on it or tripping and tearing it. Is there anything I can do ahead of time to ensure that this won't happen?"

There are no guarantees, but it helps to be prepared. Any bride should make sure that her honor attendant has safety pins, needle, and thread handy throughout the day. When you select your dress, ask what would remove stains on that particular fabric—and keep a bottle of it handy. And if the worst possible thing happens, make the best of it. Here are a few disasters I have seen happen:

- Bride's dress set on fire by her father's cigarette.

- Bride's three-foot train caught outside the limousine door and dragged through muddy streets all the way to the ceremony.
- Bride's sister accidentally stepped on the hem, causing a huge tear in the front of the dress just before she walked up the aisle.

They all survived, are still happily married, and, believe it or not, laugh about it now.

"My ex-boyfriend keeps threatening to turn up at the ceremony and make a scene. I'm afraid to tell my fiancé because I don't want them to confront each other and have a fight. If I tell the ushers to watch for him they will tell my fiancé. I'm terrified that he will ruin my wedding day. What should I do if my ex-boyfriend comes to the ceremony?"

Consider having a calm mutual friend talk to your former boy-friend about his plans. If your ex-boyfriend genuinely intends to attend the ceremony, hire an off-duty police officer as security with instructions to escort him from the scene upon arrival. Despite your fears, you should also talk to your fiancé. It's not good to hide things from each other, and you don't want any part of your wedding to be based on deception. If your fiancé is so hotheaded that you fear what he will do despite your pleas, it may be that he isn't emotionally mature enough for marriage.

Broken Engagement

"If I break off an engagement, may I keep the ring?"

No. You should return the ring and all other valuable gifts to your former fiancé.

"My fiancé broke off our engagement one week before the wedding. I have all these shower gifts and wedding gifts. May I keep the gifts?"

No. You should return all gifts—engagement, shower, and wedding—with a note explaining why.

"I hate the thought of writing notes explaining why our engagement was ended. Must I provide a reason?"

No. Just mail a simple note to gift givers saying that you are sorry, but the engagement was broken and that the gift they sent you is enclosed.

"Should I announce in the newspapers that the engagement is off?"

If the invitations have not been sent, a simple notice that your engagement has been broken by mutual agreement can be sent to the newspapers.

Canceled Wedding

"What if something terrible happens and I have to cancel the wedding?"

Just as with any other occasion, sometimes a delay or cancelation is necessary. It might be due to death, illness, loss of a job, or the need to reconsider your future together. If the invitations have not been mailed, you need to notify only members of your wedding party, immediate family, close friends, and any service providers whose services you have reserved for that date.

"We have to cancel our wedding and the invitations have already been sent. May I notify everyone by mail?"

Are you absolutely sure that the guests will receive your notification at least one week before the wedding date? If so, mailing is fine. Otherwise each guest should receive a telephone call.

"How would I word such a notice?"

It would be issued by the same person that issued the invitations. Here is an example:

> Mr. and Mrs. Sheldon Huong
> announce that the marriage of their daughter
> Amelia Tai to Mr. Lee Ling
> will not take place.

"What if it is the day of the wedding? How can I possibly reach two-hundred people on that day?"

You would enlist the help of the bridal party and other family members. They would contact everyone by telephone. No one needs to offer a reason, just the information that the event will not take place.

"What else must I do if I cancel the wedding?"

You must return any gifts you have received, including your engagement ring. If your wedding party has paid for their attire, it is polite to reimburse them for that expense, if possible.

Unexpected Death

"What do I do if my fiancé dies right before the wedding?"

In this case, you needn't return gifts or the ring, unless the ring was a family heirloom that his parents would like to have kept in the family. A note or telephone call to the invited guests who may not have heard about the sad incident is also necessary.

A Final Note

No matter how hard I have tried, I will have missed some questions that may arise in your particular circumstances. Every family has a variety of situations, customs, and traditions. You and your fiancé both will have your own ideas and predicaments. When you are confronted with a difficult obstacle or problematic person, you need to learn to recognize the heart of the problem. Then you can find the best solution for your personal needs. Here are a few questions to ask.

What is the real problem? Is the objection based on a genuine or perceived need? Is the person trying to make a statement or is he or she just misinformed about what traditions, customs, and good manners would apply in this situation?

What is that person trying to accomplish? Is the person trying to feel important or superior? Is she concerned about someone else's feelings? Is he trying to get your attention? Is she attempting to control the situation? Knowing people's motivations will help you find a solution and assist them in understanding your decision.

What are you trying to accomplish? You are trying to have a smooth, decorous, trouble-free day. Follow conventional standards and attempt to make as many people as possible happy, including yourself.

What solution has been found in past customs and traditions in somewhat similar circumstances? Because society and its practices are constantly evolving, so are the standards of etiquette. However, if, for example, your problem has to do with ceremony seating, study that section for a general knowledge of how people are seated. That should give you a basis for adaptation and compromise.

What kind of wedding are you having? The more traditional style of wedding you are having, the closer it should adhere to customary protocol. A very formal wedding would follow established procedures. An informal wedding may be quite flexible.

What would a reasonable and unbiased person do in these circumstances? Be compassionate and empathetic.

Having wisdom is being able to find a fair solution and then apply it with consideration and grace.

Will your decision genuinely harm someone or your relationship with that person? Weigh all possible outcomes. Examine your own motives and use sound judgement. Can you tactfully explain your conclusion in a way the other person can understand? Would you be comfortable being treated the same way in similar circumstances?

Many solutions are just basic common sense.

Here's an example. You are planning to marry outdoors, near the North Carolina coast, during the rainy season. Your mother insists that you should not have a tent because it will ruin the look of the wedding. Common sense tells you that you need a place to shield you from possible inclement weather.

Here's another example. Your future mother-in-law objects to the marriage and plans to wear black as a statement of protest. Common sense tells you that the more of an issue you make of this, the more attention she will receive. If you don't tell anyone why she is wearing black, some of your guests will probably just think that she chose that shade of clothing for its known slimming effect.

Our society has evolved to a point where we are all fairly open-minded about propriety and formality. In my family alone, a few generations back a wedding was boycotted by both sides because a Polish man married an Italian woman. In my grandparents' generation, the family was in an uproar and many stayed home when a Catholic man married a Protestant woman. Today we joyously celebrate marriages between all nationalities, faiths, and races. Well, most of us do.

Good manners are a combination of common sense, tradition, and the desire not to offend others. Etiquette is just a road map, and there are often many routes leading to the same successful destination.

Good luck and best wishes!

—PAMELA A. LACH

Wedding Glossary

Aisle Carpet

Covers the aisle for the processional and recessional at the ceremony site. It is meant to protect long gowns and bridal trains from any dirt carried in by arriving guests.

Announcement

A communication notifying a general group of people. Traditionally occurs through newspapers and mailings.

Arch of Sabers or Swords

Formation takes place after the ceremony in a military wedding.

Ascot

Neck scarf often worn in place of a bow tie. It is tied with the broad ends laid flat. Sometimes they come pretied. An ascot is usually worn with a stickpin.

Attendants

Also known as members of the wedding party—the bridesmaids, groomsmen, ushers, flower girl, and ring bearer.

Attire

Clothing—in weddingspeak.

Belated Reception

Celebration held on a day different than the wedding ceremony.

Best Man

Groom's honor attendant. He or she has many specific duties and obligations.

Blusher Veil

Veil worn over the bride's face in the processional. During the ceremony it is moved back over the bride's head.

Bouquet

Collection of flowers gathered together at the stems, usually accented with lace and ribbons.

Boutonniere

Flower or several flowers worn by males in their buttonholes.

Bow Tie

Made of formal fabric and tied in a bow. Worn with a tuxedo or dinner jacket.

Breakfast Reception

Takes place before noon. Usually a simple breakfast with cake as dessert.

Buffet Dining

Food is congregated in one location and the guests serve themselves. In most weddings, seating and tables are provided. In less formal settings the guests dine holding their plates.

Cake and Punch Reception

Begins somewhere between 2 and 5 P.M. Wedding cake and simple
beverages served immediately after the ceremony. Also called a tea
reception in some regions.

Cake Topper

Figurines or flowers set on top of the wedding cake.

Cantor

This person chants prayers and responses in some religious
ceremonies.

Cash Bar

Misguided practice initiated by cash-strapped couples who want
to serve alcohol at their wedding. If you can't afford to pay for it,
don't serve it.

Ceremony

Portion of the day when the bride and groom exchange vows and
actually get married.

Ceremony Seating

Traditional placement of close relatives and important guests.

Ceremony Site

Location of ceremony.

Cocktail Reception

Begins between 5 and 6 P.M. Beverages, hors d'oeuvres, and cake
are served.

Corsage
Small bouquet of flowers worn by women on the wrist, waist, or shoulder.

Cummerbund
Sash worn as a belt; it covers the pant button, top of the zipper, and where the shirt tucks into the pants.

Cutaway
Formal daytime equivalent of a tailcoat. At the waist, the front tapers gently to the back in a tail.

Denomination
Particular sect of a religious creed. In Christianity, for example, denominations are Baptists, Lutherans, Presbyterians, Methodists, Catholics, and many others.

Destination Wedding
The wedding is held at a distant location, usually in a resort or vacation spot.

Dinner Jacket
Coat traditionally used in semiformal weddings.

Dinner Reception
Traditional celebration beginning between 6 and 8 P.M. with dinner and music.

Double Ring Ceremony
When both the bride and groom obtain wedding rings.

Double Wedding
Two couples marry and celebrate together. Most often occurs when the brides are related.

Elope
Couple marries without telling their parents and others close to them about their plans.

Engagement
When you promise to marry each other, you become engaged.

Evening Ceremony
Takes place after 6 P.M. More formal than daytime ceremony.

Etiquette
Traditional and successful solutions for social situations.

Fiancé
Term the female uses for the male she is engaged to marry.

Fiancée
Term the male uses for the female he is engaged to marry.

Flower Girl
Young girl under the age of 10 who walks in the processional.

Formal Wedding
The most lavish and traditional style. Generally more than 200 guests, up to 12 attendants each, bride and groom in very formal clothing. Both ceremony and reception take place in elegant surroundings.

Four-in-Hand

Standard necktie, tied in a slipknot.

French Cuff

Band at the bottom of a shirtsleeve held together by a stud or cuf-flink instead of buttons.

Garter

Elastic covered with satin, ruffles, or feathers worn above the bride's knee.

Gratuity

Another word for tip. A bonus given for a service provided.

Gift Registry

A couple "registers" at retail outlets by selecting gift suggestions for their guests to purchase.

Groomsmen

Men in the wedding party. In formal, traditional weddings, they do not usher. Their primary role is escorting bridesmaids.

Guest

Person invited to share in the celebration.

Guest Book

Blank book that is placed on a stand at the reception. Each guest is invited to sign his or her name.

Hand-Written

Item written by hand, with ink.

Head Table

Table where the bride, groom, and their entire wedding party are seated.

Head Usher

Coordinates the seating arrangements at the ceremony. The groom decides who will play this role.

Honor Attendant

Role of the best man or maid/matron of honor. Sometimes, when the best man is a woman or the maid/matron of honor is a man, they are simply referred to as honor attendants.

Honor Table

Special table for seating particular guests. If the parents of the bride and groom do not sit at the head table, they would sit here. This table might also include grandparents, godparents, siblings, the ceremony officiant, and any distinguished guests (such as the mayor or a famous rock star). There can be more than one honor table, but it is best to intermix the families.

Hors d'oeuvres

Finger foods and bite-sized desserts.

Host

Male sponsor of the entertainment and/or celebration. At a wedding this person is traditionally the bride's father.

Hostess

Female sponsor of the entertainment and/or celebration. At a wedding this person is traditionally the bride's mother.

In-Law

Term used to define relationships created by marriage. Your spouse's mother becomes your mother-in-law.

In the Ribbons

Reserved seating at the ceremony site set near the front. For very close family members and extremely important guests.

Informal Wedding

Usually less than 75 guests. Fewer than four attendants. Everyone wears dressy clothes. Often a cake and punch–style reception follows the ceremony.

Junior Bridesmaid

Young female attendant, aged 10 to 14 years.

Junior Usher

Young male attendant, aged 10 to 14 years.

Long Jacket

Formal coat that reaches midthigh length.

Luncheon Reception

Begins between 12 and 2 P.M. Usually includes a small meal, beverages, and cake.

Maiden Name

Bride's name before the wedding, if she takes her husband's name after the marriage.

Maid of Honor

Bride's honor attendant who has never married.

Matron of Honor

Bride's honor attendant who has already been or is currently married.

Officiant

The person who performs the wedding ceremony.

Out-of-Town Guest

Someone who has traveled some distance to attend your festivities. The rule of thumb is more than a four-hour drive or more than 160 miles away.

Place Cards

Cards with the guest's name printed or handwritten on the front. The card is put at the place setting where the guest is to be seated during the dinner.

Pocket Square

Creative name for the small handkerchief of linen or silk that peaks out of the breast pocket of the man's jacket. It is worn in place of boutonnieres.

Pouf Veil

Small gathered tuft of veiling that is attached to the back of the headpiece.

Processional

The walk the wedding party takes up the aisle before the ceremony.

Programs

Bulletins that provide helpful information about the ceremony and its participants.

Receiving Line
Formed by the primary members of the wedding party to greet guests.

Reception
Celebratory gathering after the wedding ceremony.

Reception Card
Information about the reception, placed inside the wedding invitation.

Recessional
Return walk down the aisle by the wedding party. The bride and groom lead, others follow in reverse order of the processional.

Rehearsal
The bridal party practices the processional and recessional for the wedding ceremony.

Rehearsal Dinner
Meal hosted by the groom's family after the wedding rehearsal. Guests include the entire wedding party, all parents, grandparents, siblings, and special guests who have arrived from out of town.

Response Card
It is supposed to make it easy for guests to tell you if they will attend your celebration. In the world of etiquette its use is controversial. In reality almost all couples use them.

Ring Bearer
A boy under eight years of age. He marches in the processional carrying the wedding rings to the altar.

Ring Bearer's Pillow

Small lace or satin pillow that's carried up the aisle by a young boy. The wedding rings are tied to the pillow.

Save-the-Date Card

Offers basic information about the wedding. Mailed to the guest list a few months before the invitations so the guests can make sure to mark their calendars.

Second Reception

Sometimes a couple will have a second reception in a different location if the original reception was held somewhere friends and family were unable to attend.

Semiformal

Most weddings fall into this category. Between 75 and 200 guests, four to six attendants, and a reception party that includes food and music.

Shower

Party created to "rain" gifts upon the guest(s) of honor.

Stroller Jacket

Also called a "walking coat." The cut is slightly longer than a suit jacket. Usually worn in black or gray before 6 P.M. at semiformal weddings.

Studs

Small fasteners (a knob and disk connected by a stem) used in place of buttons on very formal clothing. They are often gold or have gemstones in gold settings.

Sweetheart Table

Reception dining table for just the bride and groom. In place of the traditional head table, they sit alone facing their guests.

Tailcoat

Long formal coat completely cutaway at the front waist. The back is very long and tapered.

Tea Reception

Begins somewhere between 2 and 5 P.M. Wedding cake and simple beverages served immediately after the ceremony. Also called a cake and punch reception in some regions.

Toast

Custom of communally drinking to a person or an idea. One person announces the purpose and the others raise their glass, and drink "to it." The only exception would be the person being toasted; he or she just smiles and nods.

Train

Fabric that extends along the ground behind the bride's dress. Varies from one to ten feet in length.

Trousseau

Clothing, linens, and other articles the bride has accumulated prior to marriage, specifically for use during her married life.

Tuxedo

A jacket worn for a formal wedding after 6 P.M. Sometimes it is used to refer to a semiformal coat or the entire formal wear ensemble.

Usher
Attendant (traditionally male) who seats guests at the ceremony.

Valet Parking
Vehicles are parked and retrieved for the guests by workers hired specifically for that purpose.

Vestibule
Area between the outer door and interior of the building.

Waistcoat
Distinctive term for vests worn with formal wear.

Walking Coat
See "Stroller Jacket."

Waltz Veil
Ankle-length veil.

Wedding Party
Bride, groom, both sets of their parents, and the male and female attendants.

White Tie
Most formal men's style of attire. Black coat with tails, matching trousers, winged-collar shirt, and a white tie and vest.

Winged Collar
Shirt collar has folds at the front center, with a tiny v-wing shape on each side. Usually worn with a thinner tie.

Index